RETHINKING READING

Series Editor: L. John Chapman
School of Education, The Open University

Teaching reading comprehension

Meaning makers at work

TREVOR H. CAIRNEY

Open University Press
Milton Keynes · Philadelphia

Dedicated to Nicole and Louise
my most insightful teachers

Open University Press
Celtic Court
22 Ballmoor
Buckingham MK18 1XW

and

1900 Frost Road, Suite 101
Bristol, PA 19007, USA

First Published 1990

British Library Cataloguing in Publication Data

Cairney, Trevor H.
  Teaching reading comprehension: meaning makers at work.
  1. Schools. Curriculum Subjects: Reading Teaching
  I. Title
  428'.4'071

  ISBN 0-335-09268-3
  ISBN 0-335-09267-5 (pbk)

Library of Congress Cataloging-in-Publication Data

Cairney, Trevor.
  Teaching reading comprehension: meaning makers at work/Trevor H. Cairney.
    p. cm.
  Includes bibliographical references.
  ISBN 0-335-09268-3: — ISBN 0-335-09267-5 (pbk.):
  1. Reading comprehension. I. Title.
LB1050.45.C33 1990
428.4'3'07—dc20

89–49015
CIP

Typeset by Burns and Smith Limited, Derby
Printed in Great Britain by Biddles Limited, Guildford and Kings Lynn

Contents

List of figures and tables

List of tables

Preface

Any text is in itself the product of an author's prior textual experience. The ideas which make up this book are outgrowths of countless written and spoken texts which have taken a variety of forms, including (a) conversations with numerous colleagues throughout my career as a teacher, educational consultant, researcher and university academic, (b) interactions with children concerning the texts they have written and read, (c) dialogue with professional colleagues, and (d) numerous books and articles covering a range of literacy topics.

In the midst of this cacophony of texts have been a number of significant experiences and people that have influenced my work. My early teaching experiences in the Western suburbs of Sydney taught me that comprehension stencils and reading laboratories did little to foster reading development. These experiences occurred at the time Professor Kenneth Goodman was expounding meaning-based theories of reading. The juxtaposition of these experiences, and the reading of Goodman's early work, had a transforming effect upon me as a teacher, and started me upon a path of further study and research concerning reading comprehension.

As a young teacher I was very much a 'skiller and driller', looking for simple skills-based solutions to complex problems. Countless critical incidents in my career as a teacher, and extended study and research over this period, have shown me that to attempt to define the development of reading comprehension as a skills-related phenomenon, is to miss the major point that meaning-making is at the heart of all we do as readers.

My journey as a teacher has been one punctuated with many stops and starts and a great deal of intellectual meandering. Nevertheless, 20 years of teaching, reading and research have seen my views change and develop. I am indebted to many educators, linguists, psychologists and sociologists who have challenged me to reconsider my assumptions about language, learning and teaching: Goodman, Halliday, Bruner, Vygotsky, Harste, Holdaway, Meek, Brice-Heath, Rosenblatt, Tierney and Pearson are just a few of the many who have influenced me. While the views that are outlined in this book do not necessarily represent the thinking of these writers, my work has none the less been influenced by them. I am conscious as I write this preface that I am a different teacher today than I was 5, 10 or 15 years ago, and I hope I will be able to say the same thing in 15 years time.

When most reading educators have addressed the topic of 'teaching comprehension' in the past, there has been an implicit assumption that the teacher's primary role is to help students understand someone else's meaning. That is, to find out what it is that someone else knows. Comprehension for most teachers has meant understanding the precise meaning that someone else has communicated in the form of a written or spoken text. The teaching of comprehension in turn has been a teacher-centred process, seeking to help students become better at transferring other people's meanings into their heads. Because these terms are laden with such inappropriate assumptions, I have been tempted to avoid the terms 'comprehension' and 'teaching' in the title of this book. However, education already has a proliferation of terminology. Instead of new terms, we need new meanings for old terms.

As a result, readers of this book should try to leave behind the baggage of old definitions and outmoded assumptions. Within the chapters that follow, 'to comprehend' means to know for one's self, to construct meaning and, in the process, to increase one's understanding of the world in all its textual richness. The term 'teaching' is used to represent all that which participants in any learning event do and say to help other learners come to know something for themselves. It is hoped that in some small way this book will help you the reader to make progress in your own intellectual journey of discovery, and that as a result of your encounter with this text, you might come to view the teaching of reading comprehension in a different light.

Trevor Cairney

Introduction

Those teachers who discovered this book while browsing through a bookshop, or exploring a professional library, could be forgiven for exclaiming: 'Not another book on comprehension!' For it is true that reading comprehension features widely within the professional literature. Virtually all reading texts have a chapter or two on comprehension, and complete books have been devoted to the topic before. So, why another book on comprehension? Is there anything else to say about the topic? I believe there is still much to be said.

While our understanding of the reading process has increased in the last 20 years, few changes seem to have occurred in the way comprehension has been taught. A generation of teachers has had the opportunity to share in the results of research which has shown that reading is a constructive process driven by a search for meaning, and yet most still teach comprehension as if it were simply a process of information transfer. Passages are set and questions designed to interrogate them. Little concern is shown for the reader, and the knowledge he or she brings to the text is largely ignored. Comprehension is taught as a skills-based process that can be separated from the reading of real-world texts for functional purposes.

This book attempts to challenge the traditional assumptions about comprehension instruction. It aims to share strategies that I believe are more consistent with what we know about the reading process in the 1990s, and redefines the role of the teacher in the reading comprehension lesson. It cannot be claimed that the ideas outlined here are all completely new. Although some of you will not be familiar with the ideas outlined, others will have used many of the strategies described.

What this book probably offers is a new definition of comprehension instruction. Some of you will examine the role of the teacher in the strategies outlined and question whether at times it is instruction at all. Frequently, the teacher's role is one of support and encouragement, and the major goal of 'instruction' is to heighten engagement with a text. But, despite the teacher's deceptively simple involvement in the students' search for meaning, the teaching that is occurring is powerful.

It will be argued that one of the teacher's major tasks is to create a sense of reading community by structuring an environment in which the sharing of texts is seen as important and enjoyable. Within such a community, members read and write whole texts for real purposes. Through the sharing of these texts, students create common ground in which knowledge of language and the world can grow.

Chapter 1 sets the context for an examination of comprehension instruction by outlining the assumptions about language, learning and teaching that have influenced me as a teacher of reading. It also considers the roles played by the teacher and the student in the type of reading classroom in which all the strategies discussed will be applied.

In Chapter 2, the nature of the reading process is considered as an important prerequisite for the discussion of comprehension strategies in the rest of the book. Traditional assumptions about the reading process will be challenged and competing theories examined. Finally, the instructional principles upon which the book is based are outlined.

Chapter 3 considers the teacher's role in helping students to learn about language. How does the teacher talk to students about text? This chapter examines the place of questioning, raises concerns about the traditional use of questions, and considers how they can be used to support meaning-makers.

Chapter 4 is devoted to an examination of the response to literature. Why is reader response important? What place does response to literature play in comprehension development? How should a teacher make use of reader response in the classroom?

The primary concern of Chapter 5 is the creation of instructional contexts which stimulate the comprehension of literary texts. Also, the major features of 'traditional' comprehension practices are contrasted with those outlined within this book, and the assumptions underlying each approach are examined.

Within Chapter 6, a number of strategies are outlined that I have found to be useful for stimulating the comprehension of literary texts. Each of these ideas stresses the use of whole texts, frequently requiring group collaboration, and often integrating reading with forms of meaning-making, such as writing, drawing and drama.

Chapter 7 attempts to share ideas which promote the comprehension of factual texts. As in Chapter 6, the strategies outlined require students to use many media for the creation of meaning, and to concentrate upon the reading of whole texts.

Chapter 8 includes a description of strategies for promoting the reading of younger students. All of the ideas outlined are designed to introduce reading to students as a process of meaning construction.

Finally, Chapters 9 and 10 outline some integrated approaches for the development of reading comprehension. Each shows how students can be encouraged to be meaning-makers using real texts and functional tasks.

The extent to which this book offers anything new and worthwhile to teachers of reading can only be judged by the reader. But it is my hope that the arguments raised and the ideas described will be seen as a challenge, and that classrooms will become more exciting places for students – places where reading is valued, and the sharing of insights from, and responses to, reading become an important part of enthusiastic communities of learners.

CHAPTER 1

To teach or to test?
That is the question

Introduction: Setting the context

Marie, aged 7, had just finished another day at her new school, and was bemoaning the fact that she was having problems with reading comprehension. Her father was somewhat surprised to hear this, because she was currently reading *Charlie and the Chocolate Factory* (Roald Dahl, 1967), and had been an avid reader for many years.

Like most fathers, he was not going to let the matter rest, and so responded: 'Hang on, how could you be having problems, you're a great reader. You were the best reader in your class last year.' Marie replied:

> Yeah, but the comprehension cards are funny. They give you lots of answers to choose for each question. Some of them are silly and the others can sometimes all be right. I spend so much time thinking about them that I never get finished.

At this point, her father decided to leave the subject and try to have a look at the comprehension materials as soon as possible. He never got the chance. Several days later Marie proudly announced that she was 'good at comprehension now' and that the exercises were easy. Her father asked her why there had been such a dramatic change, to which she replied:

> Oh, those cards don't worry me any more, they're a snack. I wasn't very good at them at the start, but now I know the trick to doing them. You just look at the questions, check the numbers [i.e. the numbers indicating the paragraph the answers were in], and then you go through the story until you find the right words.

This story shows how an avid and enthusiastic reader learned to cope with reading materials based on faulty assumptions concerning reading comprehension. The designers of these cards assumed that reading comprehension simply involves the transfer of knowledge from the page to the reader's head. Furthermore, they assumed that testing children's ability to perform this process leads to improved comprehension. While Marie managed to crack the code and work out how to master these cards, one is left with the question, 'Did her comprehension improve as a result of these activities?'

While there are times when people in the 'real' world are faced with reading tasks which require them to seek specific information or facts (non-literary reading) from expository texts, this is only one of the many purposes of reading. Furthermore, the activities which Marie encountered at school do not teach students how to comprehend text, they simply test their ability to do so. The following example, chosen at random from a widely used reading laboratory in Australian schools, will illustrate the point I am making. It is part of an expository text on mountain climbing, with specific reference to Mount Everest.

> *Text Segment*
> From then on, Everest was the magnet which attracted mountaineers of many nations. French, British and Swiss teams all tried their skill against its fierce perils of mist, ice and blizzard.
>
> *Related question*:   In the story, Mt Everest was compared with:
>> A. a blizzard.
>> B. a magnet.
>> C. a bird.

The question provided for this section of text simply tests the child's ability to search the text and find the right words to answer it. Presumably, its aim is to teach students something about metaphor, a 'fairly sophisticated language device. But this supposedly high-level question is little more than a matching exercise.

Any child who does not understand the use of metaphor, but who actually attempts to read for meaning, will probably indicate option A as the appropriate answer because of semantic association. Although this item tests whether they understand the use of this particular metaphor, it does not enable the child who is unfamiliar with metaphor to learn anything.

Rather than teaching children about metaphor, this question would serve only to confuse children without an understanding of metaphor, when searching for meaning. But, if the teacher had taken the time to discuss the use of metaphor in this passage, to have shared other examples, and perhaps even to have jointly written metaphors with the class, some real learning may have taken place.

Though this story is mildly depressing, it is also instructive if we are willing to take note. Marie was being given tests of comprehension each day in the guise of comprehension instruction. The procedure she worked out so as to be able to succeed in 'comprehension' was little more than a very effective (and essential) trick that ensured success on this low-level task. As Durkin (1978-9) points out, activities of this type do not teach. Rather, they simply test how well children can transfer information from one form to another. Marie was willing to learn the rules of 'the game' to succeed, although one suspects that she knew the activities did little for her reading comprehension.

What are the underlying assumptions of this book?

This book is not about the teaching of reading comprehension using methods that are little more than tests of a child's ability to transfer information. Traditionally, comprehension has been taught by providing students with set texts followed by related questions. This method comprises multiple-choice examples like the above. The methods discussed in the chapters that follow attempt to bring together a number of alternative strategies for comprehension development which do more than test students' understanding of a set passage. To highlight the differences between traditional approaches to comprehension instruction and those suggested in this book, it may be helpful to examine the differing assumptions of each (see Table 1.1).

Table 1.1 The differing assumptions underlying traditional approaches to comprehension instruction and those outlined in this book

Approach adopted in this book	*Traditional approaches*
Reading is viewed as a constructive process involving transactions between reader, text and context	Reading is viewed as a process of meaning transfer requiring readers to extract meaning from the print
Readers are seen as active participants in the creation of individual texts	Readers are seen as passive consumers of other people's texts and meanings
The teacher's role is to help readers construct elaborate texts as they read	The teacher's role is to teach skills that will help readers to extract meaning from texts
The teacher shares the meanings he or she constructs when reading, and encourages other pupils to do likewise	The teacher plans activities designed to enable students to 'discover' the meanings he or she has decided are appropriate
Group sharing and interaction are seen as essential for growth in comprehension	Most opportunities for learning are individual, group learning only being used to foster conformity to teacher-defined meaning
Reading purpose and text form are recognized as critical determinants of the potential meanings available to readers	Instruction often overlooks purpose and text form, instruction being geared to skills that have universal applicability

A careful reading of the assumptions in Table 1.1 is instructive. It should be obvious that this book advocates approaches that:

- are more student-centred;
- concentrate upon whole texts;
- emphasize group instructional contexts;
- recognize that texts vary in form and function, and that potential meanings vary accordingly; and
- require the teacher to perform a variety of functions designed to help students grow as meaning-makers.

What is the teacher's role in this type of classroom?

Traditional comprehension practices place the teacher firmly at 'centre stage'. The teacher chooses the texts, sets the learning activities (which are usually prescriptive, little choice being offered), and decides what the meaning is that students should acquire as part of the reading process. In short, all power and control is in the hands of the teacher. As Freire and Macedo (1987) and Giroux (1983) have pointed out, this is hardly the right way to go about empowering individuals. If we want to develop students who are committed to learning, who delight in the experiences they share within school, then we need to show them how they can take control of their own learning (Graves, 1983).

In classrooms dominated by traditional comprehension practices, children:

- rarely choose books of their choice to read for purposes which they see as legitimate;
- rarely write for purposes which they see as real and significant;
- are forced to read books and materials which are unlike reading matter in the 'real world';
- are forced to complete writing assignments which are unlike any in the real world;
- are given few opportunities to share their discoveries about literacy;
- are not encouraged to share their responses to reading and writing with other members of their class; and
- fail to discover that reading and writing have many useful functions in the real world.

It should not be surprising to find that children who only ever experience reading and writing as something they do at school, fail to see that it is an important part of their worlds.

Reading and writing are viewed by many children as activities to which they must submit, and books as something containing words to be consumed

(Cairney, 1985a). For these children, reading and writing is rarely seen as something to be enjoyed and used for learning. Traditional school practices, like the use of basal reading programmes, have indirectly taught children that they read in order for their teachers to either test them or provide an activity afterwards. For many of these children, reading and writing have only ever been experienced as school subjects:

- given in neatly timetabled time-slots;
- taught in ability groups;
- often experienced as a boring and frustrating round-robin exercise; and
- based on reading material which has lacked interest and literary quality.

Some children reach the end of their first 3 years of schooling with little more to look back on than a literate past featuring high points of characterization such as Pam, Sam and Digger, and an assortment of story plots concerning dressing for school, lost hats, and trips to the fire station, airport or zoo.

If we want to empower our students as learners we need to provide a rich and stimulating body of sensory experiences to enrich their thinking. And because language is a tool of thought, this thinking will be fostered through a rich language programme. It seems that children learn best when they have relationships with people who not only expect them to learn, but actively encourage and support them as learners (Cairney, 1989). The role of the teacher includes:

1. *Providing information*, if relevant to a purposeful task with which the learner is engaged. The teacher's role should not be one of filling assumed 'empty vessels'. Neither should it be that of a detached adult who allows all learning to occur as a process of osmosis and discovery. The teacher does have knowledge that students do not possess (and the reverse is true as well), and hence will need to provide information when needed as a natural part of the learning process.
2. *Listening* to students as they share personal discoveries about learning. Sharing knowledge is an important part of coming to a full understanding of anything. Teachers need to provide many opportunities for their students to talk, while they listen. In fact, teachers will be unable to fulfil other roles if they do not first listen to their students, so as to discover what they know and perhaps need to find out.
3. *Suggesting* strategies that other successful readers use. If the students' current strategies are not working, teachers need to suggest others that might be employed.
4. *Sharing* the insights, successes, problems, pain and joy experienced when reading and writing. It is important for teachers to show that they are readers and writers too, and that they share some of the same delights and problems that their students experience.

5. *Supporting* students when their best efforts do not quite make the grade. For example, as the teacher listens to a student reading orally, it should be as a supporter, not simply a corrector. Or, as a student struggles to construct meaning as a text is read silently, the teacher must be there to nudge him or her towards greater understanding.

6. *Critically assessing* the efforts of the learner when performance is not up to expectations and potential, when effort has not been applied or when the point has been missed. The teacher should never act as policeman, seeking to catch students out when performance is not satisfactory; neither should he or she be simply a 'blind friend' who ignores the fact that more could have been achieved.

7. *Introducing* new language forms, new authors, new uses for reading, alternative writing styles, new language, new writing topics, new purposes for writing and new audiences. One of the major mistakes of the 'process writing' movement in Australia was that in seeking to give greater control to students, teachers forgot that they have an important role to play in 'stretching' students beyond their present level of competence. This should not involve introducing lessons on aspects of language in a de-contextualized way, but rather, a sensitivity to student needs as they attempt to make meaning in a variety of meaningful contexts.

8. *Demonstrating* real and purposeful reading and writing. Teachers must do more than talk about reading and writing, they must show students that both are an important part of their worlds. Teachers need to be enthusiastic members of the 'literacy club' (see Smith, 1988).

What is the student's role in this type of classroom?

The instructional approaches outlined in this book are strongly influenced by interactive learning theories. Students are seen as not simply being a reflection of a genetic blueprint or specific set of environmental dictates. While the influence of heredity and culture upon learning is accepted, learning is not seen simply as the unfolding of innately prescribed traits, nor the summation of infinite stimulus response bonds conditioned from birth. Rather, learning is seen as resulting from mismatches or conflicts between what the learner knows and environmental stimuli (i.e. when a problem has to be solved). When the conflict occurs, processes are set into operation (equilibration) that hopefully enables it to be resolved. This results in learning (Dewey and Bentley, 1949; Piaget, 1966).

If learning occurs as children attempt to solve problems, then teachers have a responsibility to provide an environment which fosters problem solving. Furthermore, because learning is believed to occur as the child explores his or her world, opportunities need to be provided for this to occur. Children learn because of their natural curiosity. Children learn best from first-hand experience, by doing things, by being involved in the process. Teachers need to create environments where this is possible. This requires the development of communities of readers and writers (Cairney, 1989, 1990; Cairney and Langbien, 1989) which value reading and writing. After all, learning is a social as well as a cognitive process. We learn from others as we engage in the process with them.

Learning also requires engagement – children must want to learn, they must be intrinsically motivated. No amount of extrinsic rewards will help to turn students into life-time learners. Engagement follows quite naturally when students are given control of their learning. We need to allow students to make many decisions for themselves.

The type of classroom environment advocated within this book assumes that students learn best when they:

1. *Understand the purpose for learning.* If students are to learn, they must know what it is they are learning, what its purpose is in the real world, and how it is relevant to their lives.
2. *Feel free to take risks.* It is important that students feel safe and comfortable taking risks within the classroom. Students need to be prepared to attempt the reading of new text forms, new authors, new purposes for reading. Traditional approaches to reading comprehension effectively thwarted risk-taking by expecting students to search for a single meaning defined by the teacher.
3. *Experience varied and frequent reading and writing opportunities.* It seems beyond question that students will learn to make meaning by experiencing many varied encounters with texts.
4. *Learn as an extension of social relationships.* Reading is a social phenomenon. It is learned as an extension of relationships with other people (Cairney, 1987a). Accordingly, students learn best when they are given the opportunity to learn within social groups. 'Lone ranger' learning is to be reduced to a minimum.
5. *Communicate their insights to others.* Language is an important vehicle for learning. Students should be given frequent opportunities to share their meanings with other people.
6. *Experience success.* While competitiveness can foster learning for some students in some limited situations, in general students should not be pressured to compete with each other. Rather, students should be encouraged to set personal goals.

What are the assumptions about language which influence this book?

The view of language which undergirds the practices outlined in this book can probably be best described using Nancie Atwell's (1983) *coaxial cable* metaphor. Language is a network of interlocking systems, all of which operate systematically in real language. It has an inner core of meaning which is wrapped in outer layers of syntactic grapho-phonemic rules, metalinguistic and pragmatic knowledge, text form, social context, etc. (see Fig. 1.1).

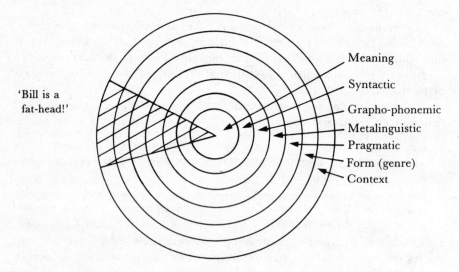

Fig. 1.1   A representation of language as a network of interlocking systems. Adapted from Atwell's (1983) *coaxial cable* metaphor.

Language requires the use of all these systems, not in isolation, but in concert. To help our students learn about language, we need to organize our learning environments in such a way that our students can use these systems in an interdependent way. However, it is still possible for learners to focus upon one of these systems. For example, students could examine the grapho-phonemic system and learn something about the way the English sound system works. However, it needs to be recognized that what they learn cannot be readily transferred to contexts where language is encountered with the richness of all its interlocking systems.

We need to remember that as soon as we decontextualize a sub-system of language, it is no longer the same system. For example, when we teach students word meanings in isolation, there is no guarantee they will be able to comprehend a sentence within which these words are embedded. Placing a word within the context of a sentence will create a new meaning. The learner may also experience problems when he or she attempts to reintegrate the new learning into the total language system. For example, if rules of grammar are learned in isolation, it does not follow that a student will be able to apply these rules within the context of a complete text to obtain meaning.

Such a conceptualization of language has a number of implications for reading comprehension. If this view of language is accepted, then we need to accept that:

1. *Language should be kept whole.* Our focus within the reading programme should wherever possible be upon whole texts. We should try to design activities which encourage students to comprehend complete texts, not parts of texts. We should avoid teaching comprehension as a set of decontextualized sub-skills.
2. *Students should encounter authentic texts.* It is important to provide students with texts like those encountered in the 'real' world. As Jerry Harste (1985) points out, if we find a text which has no equivalent form outside the classroom, get rid of it.
3. *The purposes for reading and writing must be clear.* Just as language is functional in the 'real' world, reading within classrooms must have a clear purpose too. The setting of reading assignments for purposes such as testing should be avoided.
4. *Meaning is relative and socially constituted.* Just as the meanings we create as we talk are socially defined, so too are the meanings we create as part of reading. We need to accept that there is never one meaning for any written text. Rather, every text has the potential to lead to the generation of many possible meanings.

What are the assumptions about teaching which influence this book?

Just as there are many assumptions about language, learning and the teacher's role which shape the content of this book, there are also a number of critical assumptions about teaching. Throughout this book, when the term teaching is used it incorporates the following understandings:

1. *Teaching is not just a process of information transfer.* Some definitions of teaching assume that it is simply a process of imparting knowledge from the teacher to the child. This definition implies that some transfer of knowledge is necessary for teaching to take place. However, within this book, teaching is defined as action by one person that leads to associated learning by another. This broad definition permits one to classify the setting up of a favourable learning environment as teaching. Hence, when the teacher provides books and encourages students to read, he or she is teaching.
2. *Teaching involves support as part of the learning process.* The ideas outlined in this book are based upon the assumption that the most effective teaching occurs when students are engaged in reading and writing processes. For example, rather than simply asking questions about the meanings constructed after the reading of a text, it is more profitable to ask questions prior to and during reading.

3. *The role of expert is shared by teacher and students.* Some definitions of teaching assume that the teacher is always the expert. This assumption is rejected, the role of expert being seen as something that students can assume for specific texts and contexts. This is particularly important where the reading of literary texts is concerned. Because literary texts have the potential for multiple meanings, it is inappropriate always to place the teacher in the role of expert.
4. *Decisions made to provide specific 'teaching' are based upon observed student needs.* Decisions to provide 'teaching' assistance are never made in isolation from the needs of our students. Through observation of students engaged in the reading and writing processes, teachers make informed decisions to provide help and support in specific areas.

Creating communities of meaning-makers

One of the major challenges for teachers today is to be able to create classroom environments which have a strong sense of community (Cairney, 1990). Students will develop best as meaning-makers in classrooms where reading and the exploration of its meanings is seen as important and significant.

As a researcher, I have spent long periods of time in classrooms as a participant observer, watching the ebb and flow of daily activities. Time and again I have made the observation that the classrooms where children appear to gain most from the reading of texts are those in which books, and the sharing of insights about books, is a significant part of the daily routine. The following description (see Cairney and Langbien, 1989, for additional details) of a kindergarten taught by Susan Langbien (a former graduate student of mine), provides an example of a classroom where books are an important part of the classroom world.

As you walk into the room, 19 small 4-year-old faces look up at their teacher as she chats with the group about the story the *Three Little Pigs* (Jacobs, 1969). The children sit cross-legged on a large carpet square at the front of the room, the venue for news, music, discussion, sharing ideas, and last, but not least, stories.

The class has been asked to comment upon the story and is responding enthusiastically. Ideas flow quickly as one comment stimulates another. Discussion moves from one part of the story to another, different characters being mentioned, and favourite parts shared. At times the comments relate closely to the story, at other times they are more egocentric.

The group's attention turns to the character of the big bad wolf. Robert announces 'I've got a big bad wolf and I put him in hot water', to which Louise replies, 'My bad wolf got shot with hot rocks.' However, Christian responds with a more sensitive and insightful comment: 'The wolf got hurt because he tried to hurt the pigs.' These children are a dynamic community of language users who delight in the sharing of reading and writing.

Susan's preschool class is set among the canefields in a coastal town in far North Queensland. The buildings are modest and typical of kindergartens in almost any part of Australia. A nature table is placed in one corner, building blocks of all types are available, as are easels, paints and clay for modelling. A reading corner has been established which is physically appealing. It has a brightly covered divan, a few cushions, a variety of books, newspapers and magazines. Close to it is a sign asking 'Have You Read Any Good Books Lately?' The influence of literature is evident in other parts of the room as well. Artwork displays are prominent and also show the influence of a number of books which have been shared. Group craft efforts depicting characters from books are also proudly on show.

Susan Langbien has been actively attempting to develop a community of readers and writers in this classroom. This is reflected in the classroom environment that has been created. As you look around the room, it is clear that literacy is an important part of the world of this classroom. When the daily activities of the classroom are observed, this becomes even more obvious.

Each session of the day includes the reading of a piece of poetry or prose. These sessions are often followed by a lively discussion. Independent reading time is also provided each day on a carpet area. Also, news time frequently involves the spontaneous sharing of books, and opportunities provided for response to reading. This takes a variety of forms – drawing, writing, dramatic re-enactment, mime and singing.

Even when Susan is not initiating reading or writing, the classroom is filled with literate behaviour. In the dress-up corner, children include story reading in creative play, e.g. taking turns as mother reading to 'baby'. Genevieve is observed asking her pretend mum to explain why the dog in *I'll Always Love You* (Wilhelm, 1985) had such a sad face. The 'mum' does a wonderful job explaining the relationship within the story.

In another corner, a group is playing shops and uses a receipt book to record purchases, an item that is commonly used in the home corner. 'Mum' and 'dad' are reading the newspaper, and someone is flicking through the pages of the telephone book. Wherever one looks, literate behaviour is to be found.

Susan's children are talking, listening, reading and writing as parts of a dynamic community (Cairney and Langbien, 1989). Children are learning how to make meaning as they relate to each other and share the texts they have constructed as part of the reading process. These children are not being taught to comprehend texts through isolated worksheets, laboratories and isolated skills training. Rather, they are being introduced to the world of literacy in an environment where it is valued. Reading and writing are being shared and enjoyed, as an extension of close relationships (teacher–child, child–child).

It is important to recognize that the way we structure our classrooms, the role we assume as teachers and the type of interactions we permit have a significant impact upon learning. The organizational arrangements we employ (e.g. ability groups) and our control of discussion (e.g. do we insist that they read alone without sharing meanings, or do we encourage students to share the meanings they construct?) make a difference to the type of readers we help to create.

The social context we help to create in our classrooms has a powerful effect upon the type of readers we have (whether avid or passive), and the beliefs they hold about literacy. Sadly, some children live within school contexts in which literacy learning is seen primarily as a teacher-centred, textbook-dominated activity. Reading and writing are seen simply as school subjects (Cairney, 1987a). Bloome (1985) claims that if children are asked to do the same low-level task lesson after lesson, month after month, year after year, they may develop a set way of seeing and doing reading and writing.

There is a price to be paid for teaching reading comprehension as simply a process of information transfer. If we teach reading comprehension by providing worksheets, skill-based laboratories and oral reading from texts unlike those in the outside world, then we should not be surprised to find our classrooms filled with passive, mechanical readers who believe that comprehension is a process which requires them to acquire other people's meanings, rather than trying to construct their own.

This book has as its major aim the sharing of insights which will hopefully help teachers to create classroom environments filled with meaning-makers. Within the chapters that follow, this will be the overriding concern. In Chapter 2, the nature of the reading process will be considered as an important prerequisite for the discussion of comprehension that follows.

The reading process

Challenging traditional assumptions concerning the nature of reading comprehension

Since the 1960s, there has been an increased interest in the nature of the reading process. Unfortunately, many of these attempts to describe the process have conflicted with each other, much to the confusion of teachers. These theories have varying degrees of influence upon classroom practice. Their influence has been seen indirectly in commercial materials that have mirrored the influence of this research, and more directly in the specific theories that have been taught as part of pre-service and in-service teacher training.

One quite influential body of research is a group of reading models which has been labelled *Information Transfer* theories. These theories (e.g. La Berge and Samuels, 1985; Gough, 1985) have been strongly influenced by cognitive psychology and are largely responsible for the widely held view that reading is a process of information transfer (as discussed in Chapter 1).

Theorists who have supported this view of reading suggest that it is a letter-by-letter and word-by-word process. They believe that readers extract meaning from print by processing the text in a linear way, permitting them to transfer meaning from the page of print to their minds. To do this, it is assumed that readers require specific skills which enables the transfer to take place.

Many teachers have adopted this conceptualization (most unknowingly) when designing reading activities that attempt to improve the ability of readers to transfer information from texts. For these teachers, good readers are seen to be efficient at transferring information, whereas poor readers are not. For those who adopt such a conception of reading comprehension, the assessment of success is based simply upon tests which measure how much information is transferred.

Not suprisingly, teachers who adhere to this model of reading (even if unwittingly), provide work on reading skills in isolation. Often, these skills are developed by providing a short passage, followed by a number of specific questions that focus upon certain reading comprehension skills (e.g. drawing conclusions). The example provided above from the laboratory workcard is an activity of this type.

During the late 1960s and the 1970s, a number of theorists (e.g. Goodman and Smith) challenged the assumptions of transfer-dominated theories of reading, and developed interactive theories which placed far greater importance upon the role of the reader (and the knowledge he or she possesses) in the reading process. They suggested that reading involves the interaction of knowledge-based and text-based processes (Goodman, 1984). Efficient readers, they pointed out, use prior knowledge to interact with the text, so as to enable them to construct meaning. One obvious implication of this work is that teachers had to spend more time getting their readers to 'engage' with texts.

More recently, a number of *Transactive* theories of reading have been developed (Rosenblatt, 1978; Shanklin, 1982) as an extension of interactive theories. The major difference between transactive and interactive theories, is that transactive theories suggest that meaning is not simply in the text and the reader. Rather, the meaning created as readers and writers encounter texts, is seen as 'greater than' the written text or the reader's prior knowledge. Rosenblatt (1978), for example, suggests that when reading, the reader creates a 'poem' (text) which is different from both the text on the paper, and the text in the reader's head (i.e. that made up of prior knowledge, the linguistic data pool, etc.). The meaning in this new text is greater than the sum of the parts within the reader's head, or on the page.

It seems there are almost as many theories of reading as there are methods. Defining the nature of the reading process is a difficult subject. After all, one is trying to describe a process that cannot be seen – that occurs within the head. Nevertheless, reading researchers have been attempting to describe the reading process using the somewhat limited data available to them for decades. These efforts have led to a myriad of alternative explanations, none of which have been exactly the same, but many of which have shared common insights.

Attempts to make sense of the many competing (and sometimes contradictory) claims has led to the categorization of theories under various oppositional labels. For example, top-down *vs* bottom-up, inside-out *vs* outside-in, information transfer *vs* transactive, skills-based *vs* holistic, and so on. While it is possible to group many of these theories under these headings due to their common beliefs and assumptions, the labels often mask great internal diversity.

It appears to me that there are a number of key components upon which these writers choose to either agree or disagree. However, rather than simply being arguments of the either/or type, there are continuums of beliefs in a number of key areas. These areas include the role of the reader and reader knowledge, the status of the text, the influence of text-based components (including grapho-phonic data, text knowledge, vocabulary, etc.), the place meaning assumes in the process, the impact of context and, finally, the influence of reader purpose upon meaning. A discussion of these broad differences is important to enable a clear understanding of the assumptions that have influenced this book.

The role of the reader

The way in which the reader's role is defined varies greatly from one reading theory to another. At one end of the continuum, the reader is seen as a fairly passive recipient of information (e.g. La Berge and Samuels, 1985). The information brought to the text by the reader is either denied, seen as little more than an interference in the process of arriving at the 'right' meaning conveyed by a passage, or simply not considered when discussing the reading process. Essentially, the reader's job is seen as an attempt to conform to an ideal reader, i.e. one who obtains the meaning the author has endeavoured to communicate.

At the opposite end of this continuum are theories which recognize that the reader has an active part to play as a constructor of meaning (e.g. Holland, 1975). These theories acknowledge that the reader brings a great deal of knowledge and experience of language to the reading of any text. This in turn has a profound influence upon the meaning which readers construct as they read a text, leading to multiple meanings for any one text, rather than one single meaning.

The perspective adopted in this book is fairly close to the latter. While it is accepted that readers who share similar understandings, culture and experiences will share meanings as they read the same text, individual reader characteristics will invariably lead to each reader constructing a unique text as they read. In fact, because readers change over time, so too will their meanings. Hence, multiple readings of the same text will always produce different meanings.

The status of the text

Some theories see the text as having one meaning. The author encodes meaning by using the language systems of the lexicon, syntax, semantics, story grammar, pragmatics, etc. The aim of reading is seen by some as an endeavour to extract successfully this meaning from a text (e.g. Gough, 1985). The test of efficient reading is whether the meaning extracted is the same as that the author originally attempted to communicate.

At the opposite end of the continuum, researchers have suggested that a text is simply a blueprint which has the potential to generate many meanings (e.g. Bleich, 1978). The text written on the page is not seen as having a meaning at all. It is suggested that a written text can have no meaning separate from readers. The meanings constructed from reading will always exist in the heads of the readers and will not coincide with the meaning the author attempted to convey.

This book is strongly influenced by the second perspective, although the notion of text as simply a blueprint is not accepted. Meaning is always relative and is influenced by the reader, the text and contextual factors. It is the transaction of these three key elements which is necessary for meaning to be constructed. No single component is seen as more important than another, although clearly, different components exert varying degrees of influence on separate reading events for any single reader. For example, a mother attempting to decipher a scrawled note left by her 5-year-old on the refrigerator might need to rely a great deal upon contextual information to construct meaning. The same mother when attempting to follow a sewing pattern, will be much more text-dependent. Finally, if she is reading a Mills and Boon novel, she is likely to project much more of herself into the text she is constructing.

Another dimension to the role that text plays in reading (one which is frequently ignored) is the influence that text form (genre) has upon meaning. Some reading theorists have been concerned primarily with the minute details of text processing (e.g. La Berge and Samuels, 1985), and have not considered the influence of global form upon the reading process. For example, readers approach narrative fiction in a different way to reports, expositions or parables. Specific text types set up different expectations, prime different purposes and place differing demands upon the reader.

The manner in which text-based knowledge is used

This is closely related to the status of the text. At one end of the continuum, some researchers suggest that readers use text-based knowledge in a bottom-up manner, suggesting that they start with knowledge of sound-symbol relationships, move to knowledge of vocabulary, then to rules of syntax, etc., the reader slowly utilizing knowledge in serial order before arriving at meaning. Gough (1972) holds the most extreme position in this regard, although even he now accepts that this stance has severe limitations (Gough, 1985). In other words, the reader starts from the symbol, proceeds to the word, then to the sentence and finally the text, at which time meaning is 'uncovered'. At the opposite end of the continuum are theories which suggest that meaning is the starting point for reading and directs all that we do. Other sources of information (e.g. vocabulary, sound-symbol relationships, etc.) are accessed according to need and purely in response to this quest for meaning (Goodman, 1982).

The perspective adopted in this book is very close to the latter. Reading is seen as beginning (not simply ending) with a search for meaning, i.e. the reader starts with a purpose and predicted meanings before his or her eyes hit a page of print. It is argued that meaning drives the reader to sample text-based and contextual information and knowledge. This is then used in concert with prior knowledge and experiences to construct meaning. However, it is recognized that at any point within the reading process, readers may allow different sources of knowledge to take 'centre stage'. For example, while reading a technical book in an unfamiliar area, the reader may stop and use predominantly grapho-phonic information to decode an unfamiliar word. An essential difference between this and the first perspective is that reading is not seen as a linear process. Rather, it is seen as an interactive and recursive process of meaning construction.

The place of meaning

As the above discussion suggests, some theories assume reading begins with a search for meaning, whereas others argue that meaning is not derived until print has been fully decoded. The former also assume that only one meaning is possible, the reader's role being to extract this specific meaning. However, the second perspective suggests that any text has the potential to generate the construction (as opposed to 'extraction') of multiple meanings.

This understanding is important, because if we accept it, then we must accept that meaning is relative, and dependent upon the transactions that take place between readers and texts in a specific context. As a result, readers who share a common culture and read a text in a similar context, will create similar texts within their heads. However, the meaning they create will never be exactly the same. In fact, individuals who re-read a known text never comprehend it in exactly the same way. Because we change, and the context in which we read changes, the meaning we create also changes. Anyone who has re-read a novel a number of times knows that each time they have read it, they have seen (or understood) new things. How much more then, must meaning vary for different people who read the same text (Cairney, 1986).

These different perspectives lead to quite different instructional outcomes. The first leads to activities designed to give students skills that are assumed to be necessary to extract the ideal meaning. The latter will result in instructional approaches designed to help students construct more elaborate meanings as they read, and will focus on the efficient orchestration of reader, text and contextual factors. It is the second perspective which has influenced this book.

The impact of context upon reading

There are differing degrees of importance placed upon reading context within alternative theories. One extreme perspective is that context has little influence upon meaning, i.e. a good reader should be able to extract the 'correct' meaning irrespective of contextual constraints (e.g. Gough, 1972). However, at the other end of the continuum, reading theorists argue that context has a profound impact, shaping the meaning as it is constructed (Rosenblatt, 1978).

The viewpoint that has influenced this book is very close to the latter. To ignore context is to overlook a key factor in meaning-making. Context has an influence at a number of levels. First, readers are the type of people they are because of the specific social context within which they have lived. Readers who have lived in similar social and cultural contexts will share specific meanings, and one would expect to see this reflected in the texts they construct as they read.

Secondly, any text is written in a specific context and is shaped in part by the culture and social fabric within which it is created. Recognizing this fact alone can have a profound influence upon the meaning the reader will construct as he or she encounters a text. For example, if readers approach the biblical book of *Genesis* in the Old Testament with the understanding of the context for which this book was written, and an awareness of its purpose, they will not read it critically as if it were a piece of scientific writing.

Thirdly, readers encounter texts in specific contexts, which can influence meaning at a number of levels. For example, the mother reading the note left by her 5-year-old (discussed above) on the refrigerator, may need to use contextual factors simply to determine the note's purpose. At another level, if students are told to read a novel to prepare for a test, they will read it differently than if they discover it themselves in the library and read it for pleasure.

The perspective adopted in this book is that context is an integral part of any reading event, influencing the meanings readers construct as they attempt to orchestrate all sources of knowledge available to them.

The influence of reader purpose

The role that reader purpose plays in reading is also an important consideration. Most reading theories fail to recognize that reader purpose has a role in comprehension. It is more difficult to determine the range of beliefs in this area in the absence of comment in most theories. One could assume that the most extreme perspective may be that purpose has no influence upon meaning. In other words, a text has a precise meaning (some would argue singular), which readers need to extract irrespective of whether their purpose is to read for pleasure or to seek information. This view would be consistent with reading theories like Gough's (1972), and literary theories labelled New Criticism which argue for the primacy of text. Such a perspective seems difficult to justify or sustain when one considers the range of readings possible for even a single text (e.g. a newspaper article) if the reading purpose is varied.

At the opposite end of the hypothesized continuum are theorists like Rosenblatt (1978, 1985), who recognize that purpose has significant impact upon the way a reader approaches a text and the meaning derived. Within this book, it is assumed that reader purpose places limits upon the potential meanings that readers can construct. If a teacher asks a class to read *Charlotte's Web* (White, 1952) to learn about the techniques spiders use to spin webs, then limits will be placed on the way readers approach this book and the meanings constructed.

Reading as critical thinking

Although the above discussion is deliberately broad in an attempt to provide a context for this book, it is important to outline more fully the theoretical perspective which undergirds all that is said in later chapters. As the story about Marie's experiences indicates (Chapter 1), this book is in part a direct response to my constant observation that readers are given little help with reading comprehension. Marie's story illustrates that the 'testing' (as opposed to teaching) of reading comprehension is alive and well.

Despite the fact that much research has occurred concerning reading comprehension, changes still need to be made regarding the way it is taught. Researchers have increasingly recognized that reading is an active thinking process (Smith, 1978; Cairney, 1985b; Goodman, 1984). This has been reflected in research, which has frequently assumed an active role for the reader and examined higher-level cognitive processing (Rowe, 1984). However, at the same time, reading instruction in schools has emphasized 'shallow and superficial opinions at the expense of reasoned and disciplined thought' (National Assessment of Educational Progress Committee, 1981). In the USA, a number of national reports (Goodlad, 1983; Boyer, 1984; Sizer, 1984; Harste, 1985; Mullis *et al.*, 1986) have called for increased attention to be paid to problem solving, reasoning and critical thinking in schools.

Far too many schools still pursue comprehension instruction through reading laboratories and worksheets, which provide passages of reading followed by a series of questions designed to test comprehension. Sadly, it seems that students find it difficult to see these strategies as useful for instruction. Those children who are interviewed about their perceptions of instructional practices of this type frequently fail to see a connection between traditional approaches and comprehension development. In a one-year investigation of perceptions of reading materials and instructional practices, students aged 8–12 were asked a variety of questions, one of which required them to indicate why they thought teachers gave them reading comprehension worksheets (Cairney, 1988a).

Their responses suggested they did not see worksheets as useful instruments to improve comprehension. In fact, only 15% of the 150 children mentioned the development of comprehension or understanding as the major reason for using sheets of this type. Almost as many children (9%) indicated that improving word recognition or decoding was the major purpose. For example, their answers included: 'To learn more words', 'To become a more accurate reader', etc. Another group of students gave vague responses which indicated that they were unaware of the specific purposes of the worksheets. For example, 'help me to get better at reading' (22%).

More astonishing, however, was the fact that over 50% of students gave responses that were not even elated to the teaching of reading comprehension. A large number of children (28%) felt that the worksheets were simply to test their reading. For example, one child suggested that they were used 'so the teacher could see how good you were'. Other children viewed the materials as an end in themselves (8%), commenting that doing the worksheets helped them to get better at doing the worksheets (e.g. 'so we can do worksheets when we're bigger').

A large number of children suggested that the worksheets were simply for busy work or time filling (17%), e.g. 'to fill in time'. One 'bright spark' suggested that teachers gave them 'because that's what teachers get paid to do'. It seems that the children in the above study were more aware than their teachers, that materials of this type have little effect upon reading comprehension.

Whether we realize it or not, the classroom contexts we create (and the environments from which children come) sign certain things to children about literacy. The expectations we have about literacy, and the materials and procedures that we use, all have an influence upon the beliefs children acquire concerning literacy – its purposes, its value, what if offers them, etc. (Cairney, 1987a).

Bloome (1985) claims that if a child is asked to do the same low-level task, lesson after lesson, month after month, year after year, then he or she may develop a limited range of reading strategies. It could be that reading laboratories and worksheets may 'dull' children to the real potential of reading for meaning making.

Sadly, materials and instructional practices of the closed type which teach little of value, dominate classrooms. Durkin (1978–9) found that US teachers spent very little time teaching children to comprehend texts. In fact, the limited time devoted to what was labelled comprehension, was virtually all used for the testing of comprehension through worksheets and workcards. It is difficult to assess whether the situation elsewhere is similar without a thorough study of classroom practices. However, it appears that many teachers provide children with little help in reading comprehension.

There is a need to rethink approaches to comprehension instruction. Teachers need to arm themselves with strategies that help children make meaning, not simply reproduce it.

Charles Peirce's ideas concerning critical thinking, may help us to rethink our approach to comprehension development. Peirce (1966) defined critical thinking or reasoning as a process in which the reasoner consciously makes a judgement or conclusion regarding the truth of something. He argued that every instance of critical thinking begins with the observation of something that is surprising, something which is unexpected, and serves as an anomaly. An anomaly causes a person to stop and think and search, to find something that will help to explain the unusual occurrence. For a reader, an anomaly might occur when reading the following text:

> Ralph walked up to his teacher, took him by the arm and threw him heavily to the floor. Barry picked himself up from the mat and gave a wry smile, this pupil of his was learning fast. It wouldn't be long until he was ready for his black belt.

For most readers, an anomaly would occur when reading 'threw him heavily to the floor'. Pupils do not normally throw their teachers to the floor. As reading continued, there would be a search for an explanation of how this event fits into a story about a pupil and his teacher. The reader would form hypotheses that would then need testing. These hypotheses would be based upon what the reader knows about stories, schools, relationships between teachers and pupils, etc. Anomalies represent points of active engagement, critical stages within the reading process where readers elaborate the meaning they have been constructing.

My work within a variety of classrooms, teaching a cross-section of students, has indicated that for some children reading is not an active and constructive thinking process of this type. For many of these children, reading is a low-level process characterized by a constant struggle to 'read words'. For this type of reader, much of his or her energy is devoted to working out what the words say, rather than constructing his or her own coherent and comprehensive textual meaning. Sadly, I believe that this is often the result of the reading methods that have been used to teach these children, rather than the natural ability of the readers. Thomson (1987) found that teenagers identified with reading difficulties shared one thing in common – they had all been taught using reading materials with a heavy phonic control of vocabulary. For many children, reading appears to have been a boring school subject characterized by round-robin reading and an emphasis upon word recognition skills.

Short (1986) found that even when teachers planned lessons that focused on meaning, for the most part the lessons failed to provide or encourage children to engage in what Peirce calls abductive logic. That is, they failed to encourage (or provide methods which would encourage) children to see anomalies in what they read, to be surprised, to make abductions. Frequently, the anomalies are specified for the child by the teacher. All that was left for the reader was the opportunity to read the text to see if they agreed with the teacher's logic, to use deductive logic to complete the task set. It would seem that this approach to instruction perpetuates passive readers.

The purpose of the above discussion has not been to deny that teachers have a right to point to anomalies in texts. In fact, I believe that children do learn by listening to other people (including the teacher and classmates) sharing the anomalies they perceive. However, if children are to become active readers of text rather than passive absorbers of information, they must be encouraged to perceive anomalies themselves and generate their own hypotheses. They need to be helped to actively engage with text, to do more than simply decode words as part of a mechanical process. They need to be encouraged to begin and end the reading process with a desire to construct meaning.

How important are these competing perspectives?

As a teacher, one might be tempted to conclude after reading the above discussion, 'So what! How important is it to uncover one's beliefs in each of these areas?' I would argue that it is of fundamental importance, because what we believe influences what we do in the classroom.

As has already been suggested, if one assumes that meaning is fixed, and that the reader simply extracts it from the text, then most instruction will be designed to teach skills to make readers good at transferring information. However, if one sees reading as a constructive process, quite different approaches will be used to encourage the development of comprehension. Teachers who share this perspective stop teaching comprehension skills in isolation. Secondly, they stop testing reading comprehension under the guise of reading instruction. Instead, they begin to see their role as being supportive of the reader as he or she makes meaning during reading. These teachers begin to (at least implicitly) adhere to the following instructional principles, and aim to:

1. Emphasize complete texts.
2. Provide instructional activities after a full consideration of the purpose for reading any text.
3. Provide opportunities for readers to use alternative ways to create meaning, e.g. drawing, writing and drama.
4. Connect children with texts.
5. Offer access to a wide range of text types.
6. Provide varied purposes for reading.
7. Help children to keep meaning and purpose intact.

8. Provide support (scaffolding) while children attempt to make meaning from texts.
9. Plan activities which take advantage of the strong relationship between reading and other forms of language.
10. Accept individual responses and interpretations.
11. Design instructional contexts in which strategies of successful language use and learning can be experienced, demonstrated and valued.
12. Provide positive demonstrations of reading, which could require teachers to read to them, talk about their own reading, and show them how to listen as they share their reading.
13. Help children use reading to learn about themselves and their world.

Conclusion

If one accepts the arguments that I have developed so far, then it is apparent that changes are needed in the way we teach reading comprehension. For far too long we have simply tested comprehension, and even when we have provided instructional support, it has generally been inadequate. If we want our students to become constructors of meaning, rather than passive readers of texts at a literal surface level, then we must change classroom practice (Cairney, 1988b). The rest of this book is concerned with an explication of the above guiding principles.

CHAPTER 3

Text talk: Helping students to learn about language

In Chapter 1, the role of the reading teacher was discussed in detail. It was argued that teachers need to do more than test a student's ability to transfer information from texts. Rather, the teacher needs to assume an active role as a supporter of a student's attempts to construct meaning. It was suggested that this role is a complex one, requiring the teacher to:

- provide information if necessary and appropriate;
- listen to responses to texts;
- suggest alternative strategies for making meaning;
- share insights about reading;
- support student efforts to construct meaning;
- assess the efforts of learners;
- introduce new forms of language and alternative purposes for reading; and
- demonstrate real and purposeful reading and writing.

Of central importance to all of these tasks is an ability to talk to students about text. In fact, this is arguably the most important responsibility of teachers of reading. But how should one talk to students about texts? Does it matter how a teacher discusses a text that has been read, or meanings that have been constructed? Within this chapter, I will argue that it does matter, and that the role adopted by the teacher has a direct impact upon the meanings readers construct.

Teachers can assume varying roles, ranging from those which are heavily teacher-centred and text-dependent to those which are child-centred and reader-dependent. Some teachers adopt a questioning role, whereas others provide support in the form of knowledge, alternative strategies, etc. These roles, not surprisingly, reflect the teacher's assumptions concerning the reading process (as discussed in Chapter 2). In this book, an active and supportive role is advocated for the teacher of reading. The strategies that are outlined in the following chapters are built around the assumption that when teachers talk to students about texts they should observe the following principles:

1. Students should be involved in the choice of texts to be discussed and the meanings to be examined.
2. The focus of text discussions should always be embedded within an overriding concern to construct meaning.
3. The teacher should offer information and personal interpretation only if they help readers to expand the meanings they are constructing.
4. Teachers need to find out the meanings students have constructed, and permit them to be shared so that they can construct more elaborate texts.
5. Students should be encouraged to share their meanings with each other rather than just with the teacher.
6. Questions are not designed to test understanding; instead, they are used to encourage the elaboration of meaning.

Of considerable importance to this discussion (and, in turn, this book), are the concepts 'scaffolding' and 'zone of proximal development'. A full discussion of each concept is vital before elaborating on the role teachers should play when talking about text.

Zone of proximal development

Vygotsky's (1978) concept of the *zone of proximal development* is of importance when discussing the role the teacher adopts for talking about text. Vygotsky challenged traditional notions of development, and his work has raised serious doubts concerning the popular wisdom that teachers should provide learning opportunities which are at children's developmental levels. Vygotsky proposed that there are, in fact, two developmental levels.

The first, Vygotsky termed 'actual development', and is defined as 'the level of development of a child's mental functions . . . determined by independent problem solving' (p. 86): in other words, what a child can do alone at this point in time. The second, 'potential development', is that which a child can achieve if given the benefit of support during the task. It is the ability to solve problems 'under adult guidance or in collaboration with more capable peers' (p. 86).

Vygotsky suggests there is always a difference between these two forms of development and that this gap, the zone of proximal development (ZPD), indicates the functions '. . . that have not yet matured but are in the process of maturation' (p. 86). It is the ZPD that is critical for learning and instruction. Learning creates the zone of proximal development. It

> awakens a variety of internal development processes that are able to operate only when the child is interacting with people in his environment and in co-operation

with his peers. Once these processes are internalized, they become part of the child's independent developmental achievement (p. 90).

He argues that teaching which is geared to developmental levels that have already been achieved will be ineffective, and that 'the only ''good learning'' is that in advance of development' (p. 89).

This work has a number of implications for the teacher:

1. Instruction should always be directed at a level just beyond the child's current level of development.
2. The teacher needs to implement a learning environment which permits students to attempt tasks with the help and support of the teacher and other learners.
3. Teachers have an important responsibility to observe the learning of students to determine their 'actual' and 'potential' development, and to identify each student's ZPD for each area of learning.
4. Teachers must create learning environments which provide positive demonstrations of learning for students. Students need to observe other readers and writers using language in ways that are beyond their level of 'actual development'.

Scaffolding

The concept of 'scaffolding' was first devised by Bruner (1983, 1986) to explain the process Vygotsky (1978) suggests needs to be employed when helping students to achieve at their 'potential' development level. In this sense, it is Vygotsky's concept, although it is debatable whether Bruner's definition of scaffolding is consistent with Vygotsky's theories.

In explaining what he thinks 'scaffolding' is, Bruner describes the behaviour of a tutor helping 3- and 5-year-old children to build a pyramid out of interlocking wooden blocks. Bruner concludes that the act of scaffolding as observed, is a process whereby the teacher helps children by doing what they cannot do at first, and allowing them slowly to take over parts of the text construction process as they are able to do so. The teacher controls the focus of attention, demonstrates the task, segments the task, etc.

However, some (e.g. Harste *et al.* 1984) have criticized the way Bruner defines this concept, suggesting that it places too much control in the hands of the teacher, who is seen as a manipulator and simplifier of the learning environment, attempting to reduce learning to a series of stimulus-response bonds.

While agreeing with those who have been critical of Bruner's definition of scaffolding, I am opposed to definitions that reduce the teacher's role to that of a passive manipulator of the environment. This stance implies that students will 'discover' all there is to know by being 'immersed' in learning. Such a viewpoint reduces the role of the teacher to that of participant, with identical knowledge and status (something which is incorrect) within the classroom, and ignores the important functions that teachers need to perform as information givers, strategy suggesters, and so on, as outlined in Chapter 1.

Although I oppose the notion that teachers or peers should control the joint construction of someone else's text, Bruner's emphasis upon control may reflect the fact that he was reporting observations of an adult engaged in the construction of a pyramid. This may explain the extent to which the adult assumed control. The construction of a model provides an opportunity for another person to assume joint ownership of the task. I would argue strongly that the same potential does not exist when talking about texts created by language users. Although two people may help each other to construct a text, each must make it his or her own.

In this book, the term scaffolding is assumed to describe the behaviour of any person(s) designed to help a student engage in some aspect of learning beyond their 'actual' level of development. This definition implies a number of key principles:

1. Scaffolding is not simply something employed by teachers or adults. Whereas some writers seem to have missed this point (e.g. Gray, 1987) Vygotsky (1978) stressed the value of peers in classroom learning contexts.
2. Scaffolding is more than simply prodding or prompting students to mimic the behaviour or meanings of another person consistent with their 'actual' development.
3. Scaffolding is a response to student attempts at learning. Others help as the student attempts to learn beyond their actual level of development. This help may involve the provision of new knowledge or strategies, but only in response to the student's attempts to learn. That is, the teacher or other students do not make decisions before learning takes place concerning the help needed; rather, they respond to the learner's needs as he or she grapples with learning within a specific ZPD.
4. The teacher or peers assisting the learner may offer new knowledge or demonstrate strategies, but only in response to the learner's attempts to make sense of his or her world.
5. Students take responsibility for their own learning, and they create their own texts. Those providing scaffolding support simply help them to arrive at the meanings they have initiated – they do not take responsibility away from them.
6. As Bruner (1986, p. 132) points out, scaffolding involves entering into dialogue with a learner in such a way that 'hints and props' are provided to move him or her through the zone of proximal development. However, I oppose the implicit and explicit impression Bruner projects, that this role is simply the preserve of the adult. While teachers have a vital role to play,

peers also have important parts to play through collaborative learning experiences.

7. Teachers must always beware of the tendency to make decisions about what is significant for learners within their classrooms. When teachers take control of learning away from students, scaffolding becomes simply a new form of direct instruction, and the teacher oversteps the mark Vygotsky never 'drew', but which I am sure he intended. Bruner (1986, p. 148) alludes to this issue when he asks:

> Is the Zone of Proximal Development always a blessing? May it not be the source of human vulnerability to persuasion . . . is higher ground better ground? Whose higher ground?

Teachers are more than simply manipulators and trainers. The interactions between parents and their young children are frequently cited (e.g. Snow, 1983; Painter, 1986) as the ideal models for scaffolding. It is worth remembering that what is central to these interactions is a shared history, love, trust and concern for the child's right to construct his or her own meanings. Scaffolding is not about detached teachers taking control of learning away from students; it is about support, help and encouragement.

The role questioning plays in comprehension development

Questioning has long been recognized as an essential tool of the teacher. The reading teacher has also made good use of questioning as an instructional technique. Frequently, however, their use for reading instruction has been to test knowledge or simply interrogate texts. When used in this way, questions do little more than test ability to extract information from texts and have little potential for instruction (Tierney and Cunningham, 1984).

Nevertheless, questions are important tools for the facilitation of meaning-making. Support for this view is provided both from studies of language interactions between adults and children in the preschool years, and more recent comprehension research. Research into the role that questioning plays in the development of spoken language has indicated that adults constantly use questions to facilitate meaning-making (Bruner, 1983; Painter, 1986; Snow, 1983; Wells, 1986). Also, more recent research in reading comprehension has shown that questions have great potential as facilitators of comprehension (Tierney and Cunningham, 1984).

The stance taken in this book is that the primary use of questions should be as part of the process of scaffolding. If questions are not designed to move students through their specific ZPD, then the role of questioning for learning appears limited. To fail to use questions in this way, is simply to test understanding and the ability to transfer meaning from other people's texts. Although the latter has a limited place within the curriculum (e.g. students to need to be able to read procedural texts like a recipe to duplicate meaning), it has little importance for the development of the ability to construct meaning.

Utilizing questions for instructional purposes is generally acknowledged as having its roots in the methods employed by Socrates. Tracing its roots as a strategy for literacy development is difficult. Textbooks, tests, journals, teaching manuals and curriculum documents have been characterized as having a strong emphasis upon questioning. Teaching and questioning are seen as almost synonymous. Hymen (1979) suggests that to think of teaching without questioning is impossible. And yet, a worrying aspect of the use of questions, is that teachers' decisions about questioning are at best intuitive (Wilen, 1982).

There is little doubt that questioning plays an important part in teaching. Teachers almost habitually ask questions, presumably to stimulate student thinking and test understanding. A number of writers have examined the volume and quality of questions asked by teachers (e.g. Stevens, 1912; Moyer, 1965; Flanders, 1970) and conclude that questions occupy up to 80% of school instructional time, that these questions are primarily directed from the teacher to the child, and are frequently closed, i.e. they are simply seeking a single answer. Hoetker and Ahlbrand (1969) found that on average teachers ask about 2–4 questions per minute.

Educational research on questioning has a history dating back to Stevens (1912), whose study described teachers' questioning behaviours. Since then, a large number of studies have been conducted relating primarily to practice, rather than theories of questioning (Dillon, 1982). This research has described the teacher's use of questions (frequency, rate and type), the success of training teachers to use a range of questions, and the effectiveness of specific questioning techniques (type of question, who delivers the question, when the question is asked, etc.).

Despite the volume of research conducted into questioning, doubts have been raised about the validity and usefulness of this work. Dillon (1982), for example, is critical of much of the educational research on questioning, suggesting that it typically has been concerned with practice rather than theory development. He also suggests that there are puzzling contradictions between the use teachers make of questions and that of non-teahcers. A logician, he claims, asks a question because he or she does not know the answer, and has assumed someone else does. A teacher, on the other hand, frequently does know the answer and asks the question because they believe the student also needs to know. However, because the student does not ask the question, he or she may have no desire to know what the teacher knows anyway.

Dillon questions whether such an approach to questioning can serve the purposes of inquiry. Therapists are warned not to ask too many questions because they restrict interaction; teachers are encouraged to ask lots of questions because they stimulate and encourage inquiry. Teachers use questions as a predominant technique, whereas other practitioners avoid them. Such contradictions are not only confusing, they cast doubt upon the suggestions that are being made to teachers about questioning. It seems that a lot of advice on questioning that has influenced classroom practice has been based on logic rather than research (Good and Brophy, 1978).

A major concern of reading research has been the development of taxonomies of questions (e.g. Barrett, 1976; Pearson and Johnson, 1978), influenced directly by Bloom's (1956) Taxonomy of Educational Objectives. Implicit within these taxonomies is the belief that the amount and kind of thinking varies in relationship to the type of question that has been asked. Taxonomies like Banton Smith's (1963), which identified four major question types (literal, interpretive, critical and creative), have received widespread use, and have been useful for heightening teacher awareness of the need to move beyond recall of factual details (see Cairney, 1983, for a fuller discussion). However, research concerning the role questions play in reading, suggests that the relationship between thinking and the questions asked is not as simple as originally thought.

One of the major problems with these taxonomies is that they invariably consider questions in isolation from the reader, the text and the context, Many factors appear to influence the effectiveness of questions. For example: Who formulates and asks the questions (teacher, trusted adult, peer, the learner)? What is the content of the question? At what stage in the learning cycle is the question asked (before, during or after the task)? Within what context is the question asked (a formal lesson, group sharing, class sharing)? The application of taxonomies without regard for these factors may well explain why the effectiveness of questions has been shown to vary quite dramatically from one study to another.

A major assumption made by teachers is that there is a direct and positive relationship between the type, frequency, rate and timing of teacher questions and the learning of their students. However, research evidence has provided rather mixed and at times confusing results.

Although there are conflicting viewpoints in research concerning the effective use of questions, most teachers, researchers and educators would agree with DeGarmo's (1911, cited in Wilen, 1982) assertion that 'to question well is to teach well'. One of the problems, of course, is that teachers do not always question well. In fact, even curriculum materials designed to help teachers to question well have at times been shown to present poor models for questioning. Beck *et al.* (1979), for example, found that within basal reading manuals the questions asked were (a) more random than coherent, (b) frequently focused on trivial details, and (c) of little help to readers constructing a coherent understanding of the story.

The role of pre-questioning has been disputed as a tool for comprehension development by Wiesendanger and Wollenberg (1978). Whereas they were able to cite a number of studies that have shown that asking questions before a passage is read facilitates comprehension (e.g. McGaw and Grotelueschen, 1972), others have indicated that the opposite is the case (e.g. Markle and Capie, 1976). In relation to post-questions, the results are more predictable, but still show some inconsistency. Anderson and Biddle (1975) found that post-questions had a facilitative effect in 37 out of 40 studies when the students were tested on the same post-questions. However, when new questions were introduced, the effects were only moderate, and appeared in only 26 of the studies.

The type of question asked has been shown to have an effect upon the usefulness of post-questions. Rickards and Hatcher (1976) found that questions based on a text content of high structural importance facilitated learning from texts to a far greater extent than those based on a content of low structural importance. Similarly, Denner (1982, cited in Tierney and Cunningham, 1984) found that 'higher-level' questions produced a greater effect upon learning than 'lower-level' questions.

In contrast, the research evidence concerning the use of questions during reading is more consistently positive. Studies conducted using a wide range of readers, texts and instructional contexts (e.g. Rothkopf, 1966, 1972; Graves and Clark, 1981) have shown that students who have been given the opportunity to respond to inserted factual questions as they read, perform far better on the same questions given as a post-test. Nevertheless, there is a lack of evidence concerning the effectiveness of questions used with a variety of text types and in a range of 'real-life' learning contexts.

Some researchers and educators have claimed that we should devote more attention to student questions (Carner, 1963; Gall, 1970; Dillon, 1982; Tierney and Cunningham, 1984). Given the dominance in most classrooms of teacher questions, there seems good reason to concentrate upon student-initiated questions. Floyd (1960, cited in Gall, 1970) found that students contributed less than 5% of the total number of questions asked when aged 6–8. And yet student questions are thought to play a significant role in learning (Dillon, 1982). Related to this interest is the role that self-questioning can play in comprehension development. Although few studies have investigated this issue, the preliminary evidence is encouraging. For example, Palincsar and Brown (1983) found that students trained in self-questioning showed gains in reading.

In summary, there is little doubt that questioning is a major tool used by teachers to facilitate learning. However, the research in this area is conflicting and confusing. While there is clear evidence for the usefulness of questions, it seems that the influence upon learning varies depending upon (a) the type of question asked, (b) the timing of the question, (c) the text type being read, (d) the way in which the question is asked, and (e) the teacher's reasoning behind asking the question. There seems to be a lack of research evidence based on 'real' classroom settings and ecologically valid texts and comprehension tasks. Further work is needed in this area.

One of the reasons for inconsistency in this area is, I believe, that the studies conducted have not been concerned sufficiently with the role that the reader plays in comprehension. Studies have typically involved the use of identical texts and questions with large numbers of readers. All readers have been assumed to be at the same level of development, to have the same interests, to have the same purpose for reading and to have the same background knowledge. The discussion earlier in this chapter concerning the concepts of scaffolding and the ZPD, should have made it clear to the reader that learning occurs best when the questions, prompts, provision of information, etc., are tailored to the specific needs of the learner. One suspects that much of the research on questioning has been concerned with artificial learning situations of little relevance to the real world.

How should teachers talk to students about text?

One of the best examples of 'text talk' in action is to be found in the children's novel *The Great Gilly Hopkins* (Paterson, 1978b, pp. 44–5). This story revolves around Gilly's struggles to adjust to life in yet another foster home, to understand herself better, and find love for the first time. Within the story there is a delightful exchange between Gilly, Mrs Trotter (foster mother), Mr Randolph (a blind man who lives next door) and William Ernest (a younger, mildly disabled foster child who also lives with Mrs Trotter).

After dinner one evening, Mr Randolf asks Gilly to read some of Wordsworth's poetry to him. She reluctantly agrees, finishes the poem, and sits down lost in her own inner anger and frustration. But Mr Randolph interrupts her thought:

> 'Well, what do you think of Mr Wordsworth, Miss Gilly?' asked Mr Randolph interrupting her angry thoughts.
> 'Stupid,' she said . . . . A look of pain crossed his face. 'I suppose,' he said in his pinched, polite voice, 'in just one reading, one might. . . .'
> 'Like here' – Gilly now felt forced to justify an opinion which she didn't in the least hold – 'like here at the end, "the meanest flower that blows". What in hell – what's that supposed to mean? Whoever heard of a "mean flower"?'
> Mr Randolph relaxed. 'The word *mean* has more than one definition, Miss Gilly. Here the poet is talking about humility, lowliness, not' – he laughed softly – 'not bad nature'.
> Gilly flushed. 'I never saw a flower blow, either.' 'Dandelions.' They all turned to look at William Ernest, not only startled by the seldom-heard sound of his voice, but by the fact that all three had forgotten that he was even in the room. There he sat, cross-legged on the floor at the end of the couch, a near-sighted guru, blinking behind glasses.
> 'You hear that?' Trotter's voice boomed with triumph. 'Dandelions? Ain't that the smartest thing you ever heard? Ain't it?' W.E. ducked his head behind the cover of the couch arm.

'That is probably exactly the flower that Mr Wordsworth meant,' Mr Randolph said. 'Surely it is the lowliest flower of all.'

'Meanest flower there is,' agreed Trotter happily. 'And they sure do blow, just like William Ernest says. They blow all over the place.'

This extract provides a perfect example of people talking about text and in the process being moved through individual ZPDs. Within it we see:

1. Mr Randolph providing access to a text beyond Gilly's level of 'actual' development.
2. That the interaction between individual group members can facilitate learning.
3. How a 'teacher' can exercise quiet control through questioning and comment without stifling other voices within the group.
4. That the 'teacher' is not the only person with knowledge, and that the role of teacher can be assumed at times by the members of the group who might otherwise be seen as the least intelligent.
5. Mr Randolph providing new knowledge in response to Gilly's questions.
6. The insight and responses of one group member (William Ernest) contributing to the learning of another.
7. The excitement of Trotter as she witnesses the insight of William Ernest, and her affirmation of support for him as a person and a learner.

This is the type of text talk that results from small communities of learners working together under the supervision of a teacher who has the sensitivity and insight to spot the teachable moment, to grapple for the right question, to know just when to provide new knowledge.

Test talk: Some dos and don'ts

It should be clear from the above discussion that there are many ways to talk about language, with teachers adopting differing levels of control depending upon their beliefs about language, learning and teaching. Table 3.1 attempts to highlight the essential features of the approach advocated in this book, in contrast with an approach which is seen as far too teacher-centred. These points are based upon a set which I developed in response to a forum held to discuss the issue of genre-based teaching (Cairney, 1988b).

Such a list of points may give the impression that text talk is an easily programmable spot within any school timetable, that we need simply to slot it somewhere within our busy English curriculums. It is important to dispel this belief. While talk about text can be programmed into the week's activities, it will frequently emerge from the reading and writing in which students are engaged. It should ideally occur within an environment where a community atmosphere has emerged, i.e. where readers and writers talk about text because language is important and relevant for them (Cairney and Langbien, 1989). In classrooms where this type of community emerges, talk about text

Table 3.1 Contrasting approaches to text talk

The right approach to text talk involves the teacher:	The wrong approach to text talk involves the teacher:
• frequently allowing students to choose the texts they wish to discuss;	always choosing the texts to be discussed;
• talking about text in response to students' attempts to make meaning;	initiating talk about texts irrespective of the students' level of interest or engagement;
• introducing students to new text forms as 'real' purposes for these texts arise;	introducing students to new text forms for school purposes only;
• using a variety of strategies to focus attention on text;	limiting the strategies used in questioning;
• providing knowledge about text as gaps in student understanding are observed;	providing knowledge about text as the teacher sees fit, according to assumed needs;
• using questions to stimulate thinking;	using questions primarily to test understanding;
• using open as well as closed questions;	using predominantly closed questions;
• providing inductive as well as deductive questions;	mainly providing deductive questions;
• offering students opportunities to contribute personal insights;	offering few opportunities to share insights;
• making meaning the primary focus of all discussion;	making aspects of text other than meaning the focus;
• seeking to find out what students want to know before talking about texts;	always deciding what children need to know for them;
• encouraging self-discovery;	discouraging self-discovery;
• providing opportunities for students to share insights in group situations.	limiting the opportunities for group sharing.

becomes an important part of a total cycle of reading and writing for real purposes (see Fig. 3.1).

The elements within this cycle are all equally important. Students need to see reading and writing demonstrated by their teacher and peers. They need to see that it is relevant for their needs and interests. They also need to be given frequent opportunities to read and write texts for a variety of purposes. These texts then become the focus of attention for students, because they see

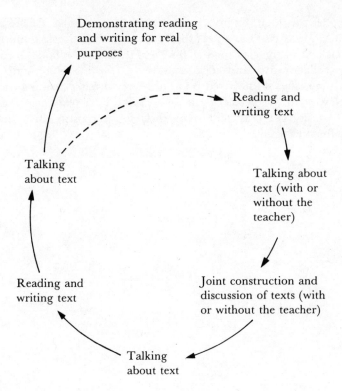

Fig. 3.1 Cyclical representation of the reading and writing of texts in the classroom.

mutual benefits in discussing the meanings each member of the group has constructed. At times this will lead to the joint construction of texts, as students are helped to move beyond their current knowledge of text, to new uses and understandings of language. This joint construction may involve the teacher working with a group of students, or may simply involve students reading or writing a text together. Joint constructions of this type will inevitably lead to more talk about the texts constructed, and in time will result in students applying these new socially constructed insights to their own reading and writing.

The major challenge for teachers of English is to make our subject relevant to the needs of students. Our students need to assume a greater control of learning in this subject, not less. There is, as I pointed out at the beginning of this chapter, a danger that increased attention to text talk will disempower students who already have trouble seeing English as relevant for them.

Teachers who are hearing the call for more text talk, should first examine their assumptions about language, learning and teaching before embarking upon changes to their English programmes. There is, as I have argued, a strong need for teachers to accept their role as vital participants and leaders of talk about text in the classroom. However, this must be done in such a way that the collaborative and social nature of learning is recognized. Also, changes must always be based upon a desire to make reading and writing more relevant to the needs of students. Talk about text must increase our students' desires to read and write texts for purposes which they see as relevant for their lives.

CHAPTER 4

Response to literature

A discussion of response to literature is a logical extension to Chapter 3 and 'text talk'. The creation of environments that encourage reader response is essential if opportunities are to arise for the discussion of text. Response is a natural consequence of most reading events, irrespective of text genre or reader purpose. It is response which enables readers to share insights, seek clarification of meaning, offer new knowledge, etc.

Although reader response is critical for all reading (the place of response to factual texts will be obvious when reading Chapters 7 and 9), it has special significance for the reading of literary texts. This chapter concerns itself, therefore, with response to literature. What constitutes a response to one's reading? Are there good and bad responses? Are some right and others wrong? Why should we encourage response? How do we stimulate response to literature without taking control away from our students? These and other questions will be explored.

Chapters 1–3 contain essential understandings for a full appreciation of the comments that follow concerning response. The term 'reader response', which has gained in popularity, is in some ways an unfortunate one. For some it implies that texts act as a stimulus to response, that readers read, are affected, and as a matter of course respond in ways clearly defined by the text. This could not be further from the truth. 'Reader response' is something initiated by readers as a consequence of the texts they have constructed in their own heads. The response is an extension of the meanings that they have made their own, not simply other people's meanings. The difference between these two positions may seem minor and unimportant, but they are in fact of primary importance. The first conceptualization of response gives all power to the author's text, whereas the second gives the reader equal responsibility with the author.

A direct consequence of the second perspective is that instruction in comprehension becomes quite different. The teacher no longer simply provides activities designed to get students to react to a text and learn how to search for a precise meaning assumed to be *in* the text. Instead, the teacher tries to get students to share the meanings they have constructed, in the hope that all members of the group can build more elaborate personal texts.

What is reader response?

Response, as the above discussion implies, can be defined as:

> any observable behaviour by a reader which follows and is directly related to a specific reading. Such responses can be either structured (and encouraged) by teachers, or unstructured and spontaneous (Cairney, 1990).

Reader response can take many forms. It includes numerous spontaneous forms, such as a sigh, tears, laughter, re-reading, a personal recommendation ('You've gotta read this book'), as well as those that follow the prompting of a teacher, e.g. a book report, a verbal comment, a dramatic presentation, a drawing, etc.

Attempts have been made to classify the range of responses that readers generate (e.g. Thomson, 1987), and have included categories like analogizing, empathizing, reflection upon self, etc. These attempts are of use but fail inevitably to account for the complexity of reader response. How would one classify spontaneous responses such as laughter, or even structured responses like a literary sociogram (see Johnson and Louis, 1985), which invariably end up falling into more than one category? Even more futile, are attempts to suggest a developmental sequence for these responses. To argue, for example, that empathizing appears at an earlier stage of development for readers than the ability to reflect upon themes is misleading. While one might observe more instances of one category of response in different groups of readers, it is highly likely that every type of response is observable for readers of varying ages.

To suggest that there are stages for the development of response is misleading. Evidence exists to support the view that the responses of 5-year-olds are of the same basic type as those of 18-year-old senior high school students (see Cairney and Langbien, 1989). It is true that there will be different levels of 'intensity' and 'sophistication' (as Thomson points out), but the same response types are still observable. Furthermore, it can be argued that variation in the intensity and sophistication of responses is related to variation in reader engagement, knowledge of language, personal experience, background knowledge, etc., and not stages of development. These variations may also reflect the reader's ability to express the meanings they have been constructing as they read. We observe the 'products' of their reading, not the mental processes in which they have been engaged; the sophistication of the response may simply reflect their inability to express the thing they feel, understand, find curious, etc. One needs to ask, on what basis does one judge the response in terms of 'interest' and 'sophistication'?

Corcoran (Corcoran and Evans, 1987) suggests a potentially more useful alternative – classifying the type of mental activity in which readers engage. One of the strengths of this approach is that it concentrates upon the activity of the mind, rather than the product of the mind's activity. The product (or response) is only of interest because it reflects conscious engagement in the processing of text (Cairney, 1990). Corcoran identifies four basic types of mental activity involved in aesthetic reading:

1. *Picturing and imaging*: building up a mental picture. Readers picture the scenes of a book as if they are actually there.
2. *Anticipating and retrospecting*: the mind running a little ahead or behind the point the reader has reached in the text. The reader anticipates and hypothesizes about upcoming events, or reflects upon the text that they have been constructing.
3. *Engagement and construction*: close identification with the text. Readers become emotionally involved in the text, identifying with characters and situations.
4. *Valuing and evaluating*: making judgements about a text. Readers make judgements about the worth of the text but also apply their own value judgements to the events and situations that unfold.

This classification is useful because it makes teachers more aware of the type of processes in which readers engage, without attempting to classify each response. Although one could comment on the likelihood of observing these mental activities at specific maturity levels (which Corcoran does), it is unnecessary and far from useful for precisely the same reasons as discussed above.

It seems highly likely that readers at all levels of reading maturity engage in these mental activities (Cairney, 1989). For example, as Cairney (1990) points out, all readers engage in picturing and imaging, but the extent to which this mental activity is used will vary depending upon the reader's:

* engagement with the text;
* breadth of related intertextual experiences;
* relevant prior experiences;
* reading purpose;
* immediate context within which the text is read; and
* ability to decode the print.

Readers may often use a number of these activities in a single act of reading. The reader engaged in picturing and imaging is at the same time probably engaging more fully in the text, anticipating what will happen next, and evaluating the worth and interest of the plot as it unfolds.

Why is reader response important for comprehension development?

If we remember that within this book 'comprehension' means the ability to make meaning, then it should be obvious why reader response is important. To encourage response is to encourage readers to share and reflect upon the meanings they have constructed as they have read. Harding (1972) suggests that reading, just like daydreaming and gossiping with friends, is a means to offer or be offered symbolic representations of life. These in turn allow us to reflect upon the consequences and possibilities of the experiences we and others have had. Just as we reflect upon and are influenced by the tragedy of a friend, so too are we affected (albeit somewhat less intensely) by the tragedy that befalls a character from a novel. By reflecting upon these experiences, we come to a greater understanding of ourselves and the world around us. Literature invites readers to 'share in an exploration, and extension and refinement of his [*sic*] and their common interests' (Harding, 1972, p. 224).

Wells (1986) found that adults who read to their children often encouraged them to relate their experience of the world to the story. He argues that doing this is an effective way of helping them direct and control the processes of thinking and language. It seems that thinking and the development of a sense of story are closely related.

Cairney (1990) has summarized the reasons for encouraging response under the following headings.

Response is a natural consequence of reading and should never by suppressed

In Chapter 1, I argued that reading is a social activity and an extension of the relationships and culture of the group. Response or the sharing of meanings derived from reading is a natural consequence of this process. We read for a variety of social reasons. For example, we read to establish common ground with others, impress people with our knowledge, find out more about something someone else has experienced, maintain a common set of beliefs and values, etc. Not surprisingly, because reading has these social purposes, we naturally desire to share our reading discoveries with other readers.

Response is the inevitable consequence of almost every encounter with a text. This may occur at intervals during the reading, immediately after the reading, or some time later, Recently, I shared my thoughts for the first time on a book I read almost 30 years ago, *Twenty Thousand Leagues Under the Sea* (Verne, 1954). This somewhat delayed response was useful because by talking about it I came to understand more fully the significance that this book had had for me. To my knowledge, I had never before shared any type of response with another person about this book.

On the other hand, while reading *The Secret Diary of Adrian Mole*

(Townsend, 1983), I felt the need to respond in some way after reading less than 10 pages. In fact, by the twentieth page, it was impossible for me to read the book alone – I found myself reading a great deal of the book to, and with, my wife. I would read silently with her looking over my shoulder, with our reading constantly punctuated by laugher, oral reading, shared comments, personal anecdotes, etc.

Although not all responses are shared (some encounters with books are very private affairs), most reading leads to the need to respond in some way. There seems an inbuilt need to share joy, pain, fear, frustration, anger, warmth, indifference, etc., with other readers. It is essential that as teachers we allow this to take place. We need to develop classroom environments in which students feel free to share these responses with others. Reader response is an essential ingredient for the development of a sense of literary community.

Reader response allows one to re-evaluate (re-live) the experience of a text

Iser (1978, p. 67) describes reading as a dynamic process of self-correction which involves:

> a feedback of effects and information throughout a sequence of changing situational frames; smaller units constantly merge into bigger ones, so that meaning gathers meaning in a kind of snowballing process.

In other words, reading for meaning requires the reader to revise the text he or she is constructing in memory. One's background experiences, knowledge, prejudices and intertextual histories (i.e. previous related literary readings), etc., all help to shape the text each reader constructs.

It is by reflecting upon one's own responses to a text that a reader will elaborate the meanings constructed. In other words, as we seek the reactions of others to our meanings, and in turn reflect upon their interpretations, we revise and reshape our own personal text.

Response is essential to help build common literary ground

As already indicated, reading is a social activity, and hence needs to be shared. Shared meanings from literature are part of the common cultural ground which shapes our thinking and behaviour. Large numbers of people who grew up in the 1950s share a literary history which includes Enid Blyton, Boys (and Girls) Own Manuals, Phantom comics, etc. While I would not argue as to the worth of some of the elements of our common literary history, I would stress that literary common ground is essential for a sense of literary community to develop. This in turn is an important precondition for the sharing of response to literature.

There are some who would claim that literature is essential for the preservation of society as *they* know it, and want it to be. I am not arguing for such a narrow 'cultural heritage' perspective – a viewpoint which does not see any worth in reading anything but the 'classics' (which they of course define). What I am suggesting is that having read some of the same books, members of a social group are more able to establish 'common ground'.

Just as books provide entry into other worlds for individuals, the sharing of responses within a group have a similar effect. As a class shares books, the individual world of each child is affected, and the common ground shared by all grows. Common ground, in turn, is essential if discussion about books is to proceed, and talk about text is important if comprehension is to be facilitated.

Readers learn as a consequence of being party to the responses of other readers

A direct consequence of the adoption of a constructive view of reading (see Chapter 2) is that comprehension of text is fostered if members of a class are permitted to share insights and understandings resulting from the things they read. Although members of the same group share common meanings because they share common values, experiences, knowledge, etc., their meanings are never exactly the same. The sharing of commonalities and differences of interpretation leads to the expansion of the reader's understanding of a text's meaning.

Bleich (1978) argues that literary interpretation is always a 'communal act'. A class has a social existence and shared values which influence the 'subjective criticism' (interpretation) of a text. Such a stance is rooted in the work of Bakhtin (1929), who suggested that language use is always subject to the operation of two distinct forces.

Centrifugal forces lead to the production of diverse meanings, because a speaker, reader or writer draws upon a unique store of knowledge, experiences, textual histories, etc. At the same time, *centripetal forces* come into operation when the shared beliefs and experiences of a specific group push towards socially constituted and preserved meanings.

The impact of these separate social forces can be seen being played out in schools everywhere. Children invariably laugh when Mrs Pratchett is out-foxed in Roald Dahl's book *Boy* (1984). Everybody can see the funny side of the children's actions in placing a dead mouse in one of the disgusting old lady's lolly jars. Everyone has at some stage suffered at the hands of their own 'Mrs Pratchett'. This is an example of centripetal forces in operation. On the other hand, one child may burst into tears during the class reading of John Burningham's book *Granpa* (1980), when the empty chair is shown (signifying the death of Granpa), because he or she may have lost a grandfather quite recently – the operation of centrifugal forces.

Within our schools these centrifugal forces are commonly suppressed, because all students are encouraged to search for the one meaning. This is seen most clearly in secondary schools, where the English teacher's aim is often to ensure that all readers arrive at the meaning which the teacher accepts as the 'correct' one. While there are incorrect meanings when reading (those which cannot be supported by the written text; e.g. it would be incorrect to allow students to assume 'Granpa' is a woman), every text is in fact capable of endless interpretations.

Permitting the sharing of individual responses allows members of a group to reflect upon the meanings and, in turn, reshape their interpretation of a text.

Response permits the teacher to make judgements and predictions about students' reading processes

The responses of students are laden with many potential insights about them as readers. Cairney (1989) suggests that a great deal can be learned from the sketches students draw in response to their reading. For example, responses varied when students were interrupted during the reading of *The Wedding Ghost* (Garfield, 1985) at the point where Jack is to open a mysterious present that has turned up with only his name on the package. Everyone is puzzled by this seemingly strange phenomenon, and therefore Jack nervously opens the gift not knowing what to expect. The students were asked to predict what the gift might be.

To help them engage more fully with the text, a simple strategy called *sketch-to-stretch* was used (for a more detailed description, see Chapter 5). The responses varied greatly and included a ghost, map, book, letter, etc. (see Fig. 4.1). These responses provided valuable information about the texts students were creating in their heads, the type of background knowledge they possessed, their literary histories, etc.

Each of the drawings indicated an object which no doubt reflected the different knowledge and intertextual histories that were being primed. Even when students drew the same object, there was great diversity. For example, a number of students drew ghosts, presumably basing their prediction upon the book's title. And yet the drawings showed a diverse range of ghosts. One student drew a genie-type 'ghost' emerging from a lamp, several drew Casper-like ghosts and others drew ghosts more human in form. Each reflected different literary histories and background knowledge.

Every response, whether it is written, spoken, drawn or displayed in numerous other forms of behaviour, is laden with information about the mental trip students are making as they read a book. We need to be sensitive to this valuable data, and look for evidence that our students are empathizing with characters, evaluating the text, building complex images, predicting what will come next, reflecting upon earlier events, engaging with life situations, etc. (Cairney, 1990).

Fig. 4.1   Some sketches in response to an invitation to predict Jack's gift in *The Wedding Ghost* (Garfield, 1985).

Providing opportunities for response to literature

Having discussed the importance of response, it is necessary to discuss how opportunities can be provided for response in the classroom. To do this, I find it useful to use the separate (but not mutually exclusive) labels *spontaneous* and *structured* response.

Spontaneous response

The intent of everything which has been said so far in this book has been to give rise to classrooms which not only permit response to literature, but in which it is actively encouraged. The first priority of the teacher of reading is to create a classroom environment in which students want to share personal insights about their reading of literature.

Time needs to be provided for this to occur. One of our greatest mistakes as teachers is to plan our day's activities so well that informal opportunities are not provided in which children can share. In my classrooms, I try to allow regular free time which can be used to talk about books. The creation of physical spaces within the room where students can mingle will also help this to occur. To encourage this type of sharing, I also do a number of other more direct things within my classrooms:

- Create opportunities for book chats. Time for a group of children who have read the same book to talk about it.
- Provide a 'great books graffiti board' on which I encourage students to write the names of great books complete with a simple recommendation.
- Plan author-sharing sessions in which students can share titles, comments, favourite parts, etc.
- Model the sharing of responses by talking about the books that I have enjoyed.

The beauty of spontaneous response is that there is no special agenda, i.e. students are encouraged to respond when and if they want.

Structured response

Structured response can still lead to the spontaneous sharing of insights by students. However, the major difference to spontaneous response is that it implies more direct teacher involvement in the business of encouraging response. Whereas spontaneous response primarily requires the teacher to provide time, structured response requires the teacher to be more actively involved in stimulating response, inviting students to respond in particular ways, etc.

The ideas contained in the chapters that follow, particularly those in the sample programme outlined in Chapter 10, are designed to encourage students to respond to texts. The teacher has a major responsibility to create situations that encourage a three-way interaction between a teacher, other readers and a text. But it is important to stress that this role must not be one of a captain leading his or her charges to the 'real' meaning locked up in texts. As Margaret Meek (1982) has pointed out, nothing we do as teachers should ever '. . . stand between reader and author, for we are parasitic middlemen' when introducing literature to our students.

Teachers and students help each other to build their own mental texts as a consequence of sharing their responses to reading. This can be done in many ways. Traditionally, group discussion has played a vital part. However, the use of alternative ways of sharing meanings (e.g. drawing, drama and writing) are equally relevant. The creation of classroom environments which permit this to occur is vital. The teacher's role in this type of classroom is vital if the 'parasitic middleman' role is to be avoided. Chapter 5 will discuss how this might be done.

Creating instructional contexts which stimulate the comprehension of literary texts

Chapters 1–4 should have made it clear that this book proposes a different approach to comprehension instruction than traditionally advocated in teachers' reference materials. It rejects the practice of formulating activities designed to improve the transfer of information from a written text to the reader, and of viewing instruction and testing as being synonymous. Although tests may teach, it has been argued that the comprehension passage and question technique rarely helps readers to be better meaning-makers.

Comprehension instruction (as outlined at the end of Chapter 2) should be based upon whole texts and legitimate reading purposes. Teaching strategies, in turn, should aid engagement, meaning-making, reader response and the sharing of personal insights. Readers need to be helped to discover the possibilities that written language has for learning and enjoyment.

The purpose of this chapter is to offer some instructional alternatives for the development of the comprehension of literary texts. In particular, we need to search for approaches that encourage readers to use many vehicles for meaning-making, and which stimulate readers to perceive anomalies in what they read.

To illustrate more fully the instructional differences between traditional approaches to comprehension and the techniques I advocate in this book, I will outline a lesson that I planned for a group of 10- and 11-year-old children. This lesson utilized the *sketch-to-stretch* strategy, and shows how the principles discussed in previous chapters can be applied.

A sample lesson based on *Fair's Fair*

I wanted to read Leon Garfield's book *Fair's Fair* (1981) to a class of 8-year-olds as an example of historical fiction. I chose this book because it is one of Garfield's simpler stories, and it is in picture-book format. Garfield is a very difficult writer for children, and for this reason he is rarely read by them. The very qualities that adult critics admire in Garfield's work (e.g. language use, complex plots, etc.), are the reasons some children do not attempt to read him. However, as a teacher committed to directing instruction at the student's level of potential development, and within the zone of proximal development (see Chapter 3), I have always shared texts that my students would not normally have read alone. To students of this age, historical fiction is largely an unknown genre. *Fair's Fair*, then, was an ideal introduction, not to mention a good way of tackling a more difficult writer.

To help them engage more fully with the text, I once again used *sketch-to-stretch*. This simple teaching strategy was first developed by Marjorie Siegel (see Harste *et al.*, 1985), and requires readers to use drawing to 'stretch' the meaning they have derived from the reading of a text. It recognizes that excursions into other forms of knowing aid reading comprehension (Harste, 1985), and it encourages children to formulate hypotheses to explain anomalous incidents in stories.

I introduced the text to the class by sharing with them the title, showing them the cover and then explaining a little bit about the author. I told them that Garfield frequently wrote what is known as historical fiction, and that this was 'the writing of stories that are not real, but which are set in times and places which *are* real'. I explained that instead of writing his story in modern times, Garfield sets most of his stories in the '1800s in England'. I told them that writers of historical fiction spent a great deal of time making sure that their details of life in different times and places were accurate.

The story is about an urchin living in the back alleys of nineteenth-century London. I started reading it to the class without comment but stopped suddenly after several pages, at a point where Jackson (the main character) is confronted by a great black dog, and discovers something in his collar:

> 'You're splifflicating me!' howls Jackson, and tries to push the monster off. He gets his hands round its tree of a neck and then cries out: 'Hullo! You got a collar on! You must belong to somebody. Hullo again! You got something under your collar. What you got?' (Garfield, 1981, p. 3).

I then suggested to the class that they might use sketch-to-stretch to show what they thought was under the dog's collar. Sketch-to-stretch had previously been modelled for the class, and so it needed little introduction. However, I stressed (as usual) that the quality of the drawing was not important, and that 'I was interested in their ideas and thinking as they read.'

Once sufficient time had been given for the sketching, I asked the students to share their ideas and, if they wanted, the sketches (see Fig. 5.1). As each shared, I asked him or her to give reasons for the choice made, and the sketch that had resulted.

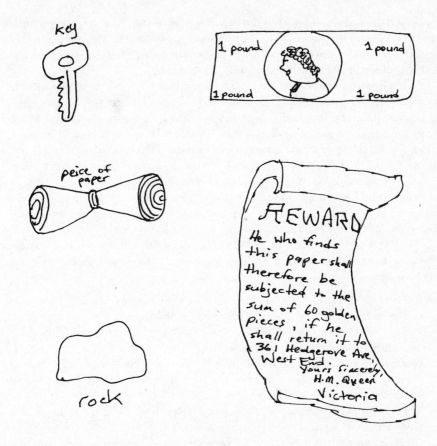

Fig. 5.1 Some sketch-to-stretch responses for the story *Fair's Fair* (Garfield, 1981).

The justifications given by each child for the object sketched were just as varied as the sketches. Both the sketches, and the justifications given, provide an insight into the texts that these readers were creating as the story was read. Carol, for example, drew a map. She suggested that it was 'from some rich person who was trying to find a lost child'. Terry drew a dog tag and commented: 'It tells who owns him.' Mark, on the other hand, drew a dollar note and commented: 'It just had some money stuck there that was meant for someone else.' Bill also predicted money, but he suggested it was a 'pound note', indicating a greater appreciation of the period within which the story was set.

Each of these responses shows that readers formulate different hypotheses as they read, and hence, create different texts. The sharing of these personal texts helps each student to construct more elaborate texts as the reading continues. Once all of the students who had wanted to share had done so, I continued to read the story until the object was revealed. The accuracy of their predictions was then discussed and predictions were made about what might happen next in the story. At this point, the lesson ended, and the students were told that the story would be continued the next day.

This lesson was planned and implemented with a number of purposes in mind. First, it permitted children to learn more about the text by sharing their responses. The sharing of different interpretations permits each child to expand the range of plausible hypotheses that can be generated as they read. Secondly, listening to others refer back to aspects of the text to justify sketches, allows each child to embellish his or her own mental text. Thirdly, participants in lessons of this type are learning language, learning through language and learning about language (Halliday, 1975). Finally, the engagement of a reader with the text is enhanced as he or she returns to the text to complete the reading (or in this case, to listen to it).

The rest of the story was read over another three lessons (see Cairney, 1990, for the complete details of this programme). In these lessons, students were asked to:

- Reflect upon the images Garfield creates with expressions like 'It glared and growled while the snow flakes fried on its nose'.
- Predict what might be inside the mansion that Jackson eventually finds and enters using the mysterious key.
- Discuss in small groups whether it is the dog who keeps leaving food mysteriously each night in the deserted mansion where Jackson and another urchin take up temporary residence.
- Reflect upon the impact the complete story had on their feelings and emotions, and what memories it stimulated.
- Meet in groups to consider the appropriateness of the ending and the qualities of the major characters, Jackson and Lillypolly.

Major differences between traditional comprehension approaches and those described in this book

The differences between the lessons planned for this book and lessons utilizing traditional comprehension teaching methods (i.e. the use of activities which require the reading of a short text and the completion of a series of questions afterwards), should be apparent to the reader. For convenience, the major differences are summarized in Table 5.1.

As stated at the outset of this book, traditional classroom practices have provided children with very little assistance when trying to make meaning from texts. At best, much of what we have done in the name of reading comprehension has been little more than simple testing of recall. At worst it has involved the *testing* (as opposed to teaching) of the ability to infer and comment critically upon text.

Table 5.1 The major differences between traditional approaches to comprehension and those used in this book

Strategies used in this book	*Passage, questions, test method*
• Varied responses are invited and encouraged	Typically requires only one correct response
• The child is encouraged to see anomalies in what is read and formulate hypotheses	At best, it suggests an hypothesis for the child to test, but often only requires a text search
• Readers are permitted and encouraged to share responses and learn from each other	Is often completed as an individual activity which prevents sharing
• Readers are encouraged to reformulate hypotheses as part of the reading process	Provides little opportunity for the reformation of hypotheses, because the task is often set immediately after reading
• Readers are encouraged to focus upon large parts of (and often the whole) text	Usually focuses upon small sections of the text, sometimes no more than a sentence

The suggestions outlined above have been provided to show that there is an alternative to traditional comprehension instruction. The creative teacher is capable of devising many activities of this type. However, when choosing additional activities to use with children, it is important to choose strategies which:

- help readers create meaning as texts are encountered;
- require readers to construct a coherent understanding of whole texts;
- encourage excursions into other forms of meaning making (such as writing, drawing, dramatization, etc.);
- permit readers to learn from each other as they share the meanings they have created as a result of their reading; and
- stimulate readers to think abductively, formulating hypotheses as they read (Cairney, 1988b).

Above all, we need to help children to stop focusing only on the words, and move their attention to the characters, the plot, the suspense, the humour. We want them to start creating complete texts as they read, not fragments of texts. We want them to see anomalies, formulate hypotheses and test them out against their experiences (Cairney, 1988b). Our students need to 'build bridges between the new and the known' (Pearson and Johnson, 1978, p. 24). We want our young readers to say: 'Aha, I didn't see it that way.' 'No, I don't agree with that.' 'Don't you think another way to look at it is . . . ?'

Responses of this type show that readers are trying to construct, re-construct and embellish their own texts as they read. Just as Graves (1983) suggested that teachers ought to give control of writing to children, so, in the same way, teachers must encourage them to take control of their reading. We need to develop readers who create elaborate texts as they read, not readers who search for an answer – or a meaning – that they think the teacher, or the worksheet, requires. Chapter 6 will outline strategies like sketch-to-stretch which I have found effective for achieving these purposes.

Strategies for developing the comprehension of literary texts

Before describing each of the strategies, it is important to stress they are not a 'hotchpotch' of activities to be used indiscriminately. Each should only be used if appropriate for a particular group of students and a specific text. You may find, for example, that sketch-to-stretch (outlined in Chapter 5) is a useful way to heighten the engagement of some students with text. However, other students may find that it is less helpful, preferring to talk or write about the text. Also, some texts lend themselves to particular strategies, whereas others do not. For example, texts with a strong sense of place, like *The Wind in the Willows* (Grahame, 1908), are well suited to story mapping (discussed in detail below), whereas it proves unsuitable with texts which lack a strong setting.

If each of the strategies which follow is to be used effectively, it is also important for teachers to accept the roles assigned to them in Chapter 1, and the assumptions concerning language and learning. The use of the ideas outlined in any other instructional context will ensure that students once again receive little help with reading comprehension. In the wrong hands, all of the strategies discussed have the potential to impose the teacher's meaning upon the student. This is to be avoided at all costs.

Collaborative stories

Introduction

I have devised the term 'collaborative story' to describe an activity requiring students to create their own stories in response to a non-text version of a picture book. I use the label 'collaborative' because the strategy requires collaboration between the original and the new (child) author. I have used it successfully with children of varying abilities. For example, I have seen non-readers aged 7 years make great strides towards independence using this technique, and talented 12-year-olds 'stretched'.

Its great strength as a strategy is that it gives children the opportunity to create meaning at the text level. In doing this, they become more aware of story structure and character development, rather than just sentence and word meaning. It also has the advantage that it can be used to introduce students to texts well beyond their levels of 'actual' development (see Chapter 3), taking advantage of each child's zone of proximal development.

Procedure

To use the strategy, one needs to create a no-text version of a picture book. Although a number of books of this type are commercially available, it is easy to create your own, and for the reasons outlined above, preferable. I do this in three different ways:

- Take old picture books and cover the text with adhesive labels or white masking tape (you need a second copy with the text kept intact).
- Place strips of paper over the text, holding them in place with paper clips. Alternatively, you can use note pads with a gummed edge.
- Place strips of paper over the text and photocopy selected pages.

Once the no-text version of the book is complete, the teacher shares the original story with the child, group or class. With less proficient readers (e.g. kindergarten or non-readers), the teacher reads it to them, whereas with more proficient readers they might read it themselves. Once the text has been read (not necessarily the same day), the students are ready to produce their own versions. The decision may be made to reproduce a similar story using the students' language (without looking back at the text), or the children may decide to try to produce a completely different version of the story.

The role of the teacher in this composing process will vary, depending upon the ability of the children and the size of the group with which the teacher is working. For example, if the teacher is working with young readers, he or she will need to scribe the text for them (although they might to do their own drafts) while they compose. More proficient readers might work independently or in groups, with the teacher's role reduced significantly. No matter how teachers use the activity, the composing should be done by the children.

The activity ends when the new text is shared with other readers. Some children might then like to go back to the original text to see how the new text is different. Each text that is produced in this way is then read and re-read by the pupil to different audiences, and silently as often as he or she wishes.

Variations to this strategy

A useful variation is to use the pictures from a text which the students have not seen before. Although this changes the nature of the lesson, the children still have to use a similar knowledge of language to construct the text. What this variation offers, is complete freedom from the constraints of the original text stored in memory.

Text shuffle

Introduction

This is an old strategy which has been used successfully by many teachers. It involves cutting a text into pieces (using logical divisions based on meaning) and presenting the text segments to individual children or small groups of 4–6. As with collaborative story, it requires the reader to create meaning at the text level. In particular, it creates a need for the use of story structures, which may or may not have been intuitively learned through the experience of literature.

Procedure

To use this strategy, I usually select a text of 200–500 words. Although the strategy can be used with non-literary texts, I prefer to do it with narrative texts. Preparing the materials is relatively easy. Picture books or short stories are ideal.

After typing the text, it should be cut into logical segments. These segments are then glued on to pieces of cardboard of uniform size and each child is provided with one (if working in groups). The group is then asked to try and reconstruct the text. At first the teacher might need to help them by asking questions such as 'Who thinks they have the first part?' 'Why do you know that piece comes next?' However, it does not take long for most children to learn how to negotiate the meaning without assistance. If this technique is used with individuals (which in my opinion is not as useful), then each child will need to be provided with all of the pieces. Because individuals lack the collective wisdom of a group, shorter and simpler texts with less segments will probably need to be used.

Variations to this strategy

As a variation to this activity, I often provide the group with one or two blank cards (deliberately leaving out sections of the text). The group must also place the blank cards in position and write the missing text segments themselves.

Story frames

Introduction

Story frames are a form of probed text recall (Cairney, 1985b). The story frame is a skeletal outline of the text – a sort of story-level cloze. The skeleton contains just enough information to probe a child's recall of a story he or she has constructed and stored in memory. However, this technique is not designed to test memory of text; its aim is to help readers construct a coherent understanding of a text. One of the difficulties that some readers face is not being able to organize the information generated by the text. They are only able to remember isolated segments of a text that they have created while reading. This technique helps them to construct a coherent representation of the text.

Procedure

The frame should not be too detailed, otherwise the activity becomes far too restrictive. Children can complete this individually or in small groups. Once again, group collaboration is preferable.

The presentation of the original text can be done in a variety of ways. For example, if a picture book is selected which is beyond the children's current reading level, the teacher will have to read it to them. On the other hand, you might use a text which is written within their reading capabilities, then they can read it themselves.

After the story has been read, each child attempts to recall the text they have constructed and stored in memory. If working in groups, each member suggests something that can be placed in each slot. Once the frame is complete (see Fig. 6.1), it is read right through and the content discussed.

Individually, children are encouraged to consider how accurately they feel the frame reflects the meaning they created as they read the original story. A useful extension to this technique is to ask the children to create story frames for other children to complete.

Variations to this strategy

Story frames can take a variety of forms. Whereas the above is a simple narrative plot summary, it is also possible to design the frame for one incident in the story, a description of one character, or an outline of a setting. In each case, the demands of the task are different, but the principles upon which it is based are the same.

Michael Magee lived ...on the outer Barcoo........
..with his family... It was way out in .....
..the bush..........................
One day ..he... decided that his son needed to be
Christened because they hadn't got around to it
Now his son   was...ten years old when...a .....
.travelling preacher came by and agreed to..
..do it.................................
But it just so happened that .the boy heard them....
.talking and thought Christening was a bit
.like branding sheep...........
So straight away .he took off so they..........
..couldn't catch him.............,
but ..he made ....a big ...mistake ....and.......
..hid in ....a log... The preacher told
...Mike to poke him with a stick to....
.get him to come out so he could be.....
..christened.. Which is what he did.....
....
and his parents ...waited to see if he'd....
.come out. The problem was when he....
.raced out the preacher realized they had no..
.name picked out for him.
The priest decided ...there was no time to...
.waste so he took a flask of whisky...
.from his pocket and threw it at him..
And so ...that's how he became known as....
.Maginnis because that's what the
.whisky was called..........................

Fig. 6.1 A story frame written for *A Bush Christening* (Paterson, 1976).

Story transformation

Introduction

This activity is a modification of one I have previously referred to as 'lap stories' (Cairney, 1985b). In using a new label I am simply widening its scope. Lap stories require two students to reconstruct and present a story to an audience together. Both students create concrete visual props to support the reading of the text, which might take the form of three-dimensional plasticine models, drawings, etc. When the story is related to the audience, one child reads while the other displays the appropriate prop.

This technique aims to encourage children to use alternative ways to make meaning. It is based upon the belief that using non-written methods to create meaning helps the reader to construct a more enriched personal representation of the text. It also helps readers to learn more about written language as part of the process.

Procedure

The essential purpose of story transformation is to encourage students to reconstruct a text that will then be shared with a larger audience. The text may have been read to the students by the teacher or it could have been read independently. Following the reading of the story, the students are asked to provide a verbal retelling of the story, with props to support their presentation. For example, they might use silhouettes on an overhead projector, a time line, dramatization, mime, puppetry, etc. By encouraging the children to experiment with other methods of making meaning, they are then able to share the meaning they have created with other children.

It is essential to demonstrate how story transformation works. This is usually done with the participation of the class. For example, 6-year-olds can prepare the silhouettes for the text 'There was an old lady who swallowed a fly' (Adams, 1973). The story can then be told by one or two members of the class, others manipulating the silhouettes.

To make group participation easier, an overhead projector can be set up behind a white sheet, thus providing a perfect screen for the projection of the silhouettes. Alternatively, the children could be asked to draw some pictures and cut them out. These could then be displayed on a conventional screen (or even a white wall) by means of an overhead projector.

Variations to this strategy

The part that the original text plays in this type of lesson can vary greatly. For example, if drama is being used to support the story, the text may be modified to provide a script. In this case, students might work in groups to produce a written script. It is also possible for students to produce a written retelling of the text for sharing using the original for guidance. Each of these, and other variations, create differing needs to revisit the written text, whereas the above involves students simply retelling the story from memory.

Character mug sheets

Introduction

The character mug is a simple strategy designed to focus the students' attention upon the personalities of specific characters in a text (Cairney, 1983). Its use encourages children to consider not only the personality traits of the character, but the relationships between different characters. Although many readers (especially avid readers) need little help to concentrate upon the characterization in a text, this technique encourages others to reflect upon characters in a way which may not have occurred to them previously.

Procedure

Mug sheets can be used with any narrative text that children have listened to or have read. Although the composition of the mug sheet can vary, I have found the following format to be particularly useful. To demonstrate the use of mug sheets, it is appropriate to use a character that all the children are familiar with, one that is preferably from a piece of literature that the teacher has already read to the children. It is also useful to show the class how mug sheets can take a number of forms. For example, I often demonstrate the construction of a mug sheet based upon fact, and one which involves the 'stretching of the truth'.

It matters little whether the children decide to create mug sheets based purely upon the traits and the events contained in the story, or decide to present a light-hearted interpretation of the character (see Fig. 6.2). In both cases, the reader needs to know the character.

Once the children have created their mug sheets, they should be given the opportunity to share them with other members of the class. This is not only extremely enjoyable, but it gives students a chance to hear how others have represented the same, or a different, character from the same book.

Variations to this strategy

There are a number of possible variations to this strategy. The format can be

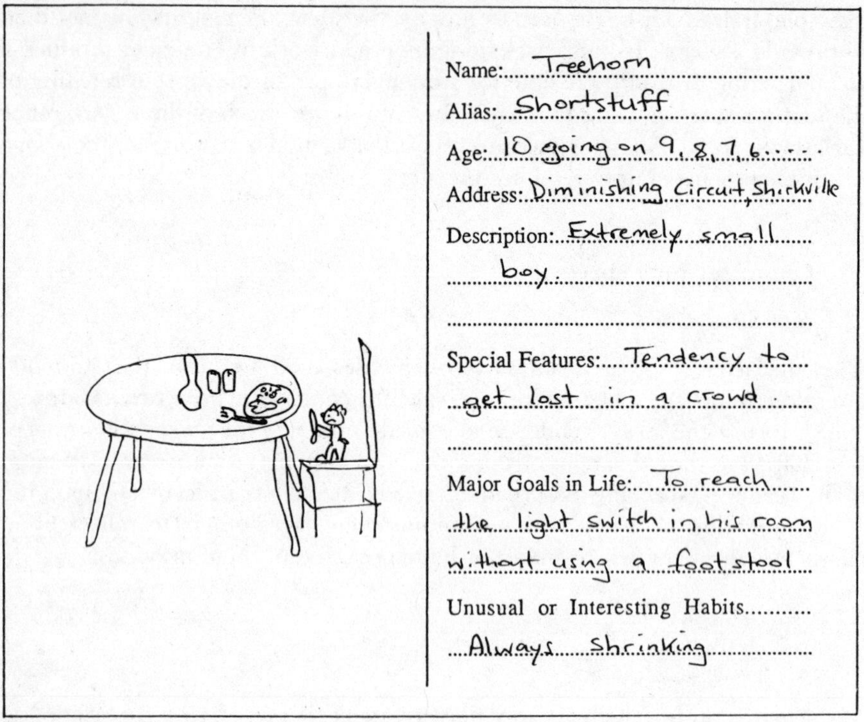

Name: Treehorn
Alias: Shortstuff
Age: 10 going on 9, 8, 7, 6......
Address: Diminishing Circuit, Shirkville
Description: Extremely small boy.

Special Features: Tendency to get lost in a crowd.

Major Goals in Life: To reach the light switch in his room without using a footstool
Unusual or Interesting Habits.......... Always Shrinking

Fig. 6.2   A mug sheet for the character Treehorn in *The Shrinking of Treehorn* (Heide, 1975).

changed simply by adding or deleting specific categories of information. For example, one might add categories like 'favourite TV programme', 'how he/she spends his/her spare time', 'last seen', and so on. A finger-print section could even be added (using a stamp pad). The mug sheet can also be changed into a wanted poster, and then displayed around the room. This simple change in format requires the students to be aware of the need to catch people's attention, and present information clearly.

Written conversation with a character

Introduction

This strategy is based on 'written conversation', which has been used widely in recent years to encourage young writers to produce a written dialogue with a friend. However, in this case, students are asked to have a dialogue with a character from a book they have been reading. The purpose of this is to encourage students to focus upon a specific character, and try to understand the way he or she thinks, acts, talks and writes.

Procedure

I begin by modelling the strategy for the class. This is done by selecting a character that all the students know and beginning a conversation with him or her on an overhead projector or blackboard as follows:

Carlie:	I'm sick and tired of living here Mrs Mason, why do you continue to deliberately try to annoy me by fussing over me? I hate people who fuss.
Mrs Mason:	Carlie, I'm only trying to look after you and Harvey and Thomas J. the way I think I should. It seems to me that you could do with a bit of attention for a change.
Carlie:	What the hell's that supposed to mean?
Mrs Mason:	Don't cuss like that child. I mean, I just want to make sure you all have a little love and care.
Carlie:	Well don't worry about me. I don't need to be another one of your girl scout do good projects. I've told you before I don't intend to end up as the 18th face on your mantelpiece.
Mrs Mason:	Have it your way Carlie, You won't end up on any mantelpiece if you don't want to.

(a written conversation between Carlie and Mrs Mason in Betsy Byars' *The Pinballs*, 1977).

Usually, one begins such a conversation with a statement followed by a question. The question is designed to invite a response. I then respond on behalf of the character, who in turn shares something and perhaps asks a question.

Once the dialogue is well under way, I encourage the class to join in by suggesting what might be written next. Then, perhaps, specific students come to the front and assume the role of one of the characters.

After this has been demonstrated, I break the class into pairs and ask them to select the role they will perform. Will they be a character, or an interested person engaging in dialogue? I find that some of the most useful conversations are between two different characters in the same story. If this approach is used, each child assumes the role of a different character.

Once the conversations are completed, the students are encouraged to share them in small groups.

Variations to this strategy

There are a number of variations to this strategy. One of the most enjoyable is to ask the students to assume the roles of characters from two different books, e.g. *The BFG* from the book of the same name (Dahl, 1982), and *Jack* from the story of *Jack and the Beanstalk* (Lang, 1969). These characters then converse with each other about things which might be of mutual interest.

Never-ending story

Introduction

This technique is an integrated reading and writing strategy. The children are provided with the beginning of a story which they must continue to write, until they are told to pass the story on to another child for it to be continued. Like written conversation, this technique requires the child to read and write in an interactive way: first reading, then writing, reading, then writing, and so on. An added advantage over written conversation is that it requires the reader/writer to construct meaning for extended texts (both through reading and writing). Each time a new text is passed on to the next student, it is necessary for him or her to read the text that has already been written, predict what the author was trying to create and plan how to extend the text. In a sense, this activity forces the reader to 'read like a writer' in a way difficult to achieve simply through conventional writing lessons.

Procedure

I always introduce this activity by modelling it on an overhead projector. After displaying the beginning of the story (selected from any piece of literature), I write the next section of the text. After writing several sentences I stop, read the text out aloud, and ask the group to suggest what might come next. I then take someone's suggestion and write the next section of the text. I continue in this way until the text is completed to the group's satisfaction.

When children attempt this activity, the format can vary greatly. However, I will describe one format which has worked particularly well for me. Before asking the group to start writing, I explain that they will only be given a limited amount of time to write something, and that they will then have to pass it on to another writer. I tell them that the text will be passed around until all members of the group have contributed something to it, and the last person has completed the story. If this activity is used with the whole class, the number of children who contribute to the text will need to be limited. Ideally, the activity should be used with groups of 4–8 children.

The story's beginning should only be two or three sentences long. It should introduce a character, set a little of the scene, and perhaps even provide some initiating event. Each child in the group receives a copy of the story's beginning, and is then asked to start writing. After about 3 minutes, they pass the text on. No matter how much time the child is allowed, they must always be warned beforehand that they are going to be asked to stop writing. The only variation to this is that one should provide extra time for the ending to the text. In fact, I normally allow each child to continue to write until they are satisfied with the ending.

Once each piece has been finished (see Fig. 6.3), it is returned to the person who started it and it is then shared with the group. One alternative is to ask the person who finished the story to read it to the group.

NEVER-ENDING STORY

Max squeezed slowly through the narrow opening. His
heart was beating like a bass drum. He couldn't help but
wonder how he got himself into this si tua tion.

His friends had dared him to go into old Mrs Jonstons
creepy House. People say it is Haunted. A man died there once
and has never been found after his death. Now old Mrs Jonston
loves that house and is a bit horrible at times. Some
people go in and never come out again. Was
he frightened? He thought to himself "now I got to
(Penny) calm down if I'm going to get that ten dollars
they said they'd give me." Max went slowly through
the front gate, it creaked when he shut it.

Mrs Johnston was out. Max carefully opened the front
door. A cat leapt in front of him.

(Georgia) "Augh!" exclaimed Max but he quickly calmed down
and he strolled on. He found a cupboard. Max leaned in
and discovered there was no floor in there, just a
deep hole which Max fell into.

he landed in a net. The net
tore. Max fell into a crocodile
swamp but luckily he fell on to a
rock and the crocks couldn't get
(Nicolette) him. He stayed there and then tried
to climb up. He couldn't

He struggled to climb out off the rock but
failed. His jacket was weighing him down fell down into
(Amanda) He sank deeper and deeper till finally he the swamp.
drowned and died a slow, painfull death...

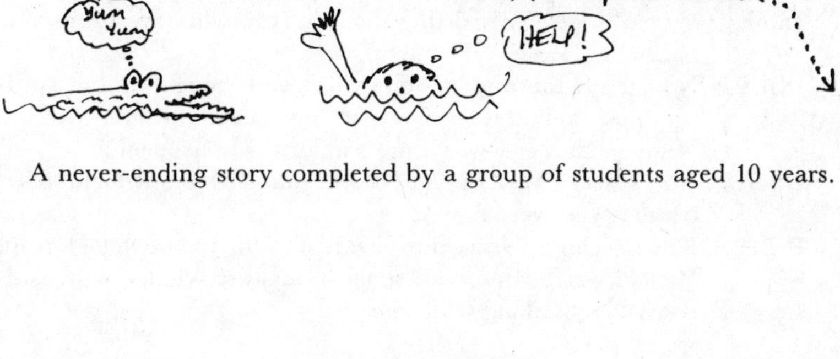

Fig. 6.3   A never-ending story completed by a group of students aged 10 years.

Character interviews

Introduction

This activity is a highly creative form of literary response. It requires a thorough understanding and appreciation of the text, and encourages the reader to 'get inside the character', as well as elaborating upon the text. By placing the students in situations that require them to interview a character, they are forced to reflect upon the qualities that the character possesses and the way he or she thinks. The strategy also encourages students to 're-visit' the text to clarify what they know about the character in question.

Procedure

As with many of the other strategies discussed, I always model it first. I explain that the aim is to interview a character from a story that they know well. I take a story that I have shared with them, select a character (and give my reasons for the choice), and then proceed to act out an interchange between a detached interviewer (i.e. someone who is not part of the story) and that character.

Once I have demonstrated how the interview might unfold, I ask the children to brainstorm characters from stories they have read who could be interviewed. I then explain to them that their job is not to retell the story, but to take one aspect of it and use it for the interview, as if it were part of real life. I then split the group into pairs, each of which is encouraged to select a character, decide who will fill the separate roles of interviewer and interviewee, and then proceed to prepare an interview, recording all questions and answers. The following is a character interview prepared for Elizabeth in *The Paper Bag Princess* (Munsch, 1980) by Clementine, aged 12:

Inter.: We welcome warmly the Paper Bag Princess. As you may recall, she heroically saved her prince from the dragon's lair. Tell me, did you plan, right from the beginning to tire out the dragon so you could save the prince?

P.B.P.: Well, it was just one of those 'on-the-spur-of-the-moment' ideas.

Inter.: Weren't you worried that the dragon might have burnt your scanty paper bag dress?

P.B.P.: Now that I think of it, I don't believe I thought of it at all. Indeed, I was lucky to find it to wear when my palace burnt down. The burning of my clothes etc, was a most unfortunate happening.

Inter.: Ah, I see. Weren't you downhearted when Ronald rejected you because you were a mess?

P.B.P.: I was feeling a little downhearted at first, but then I realized that Ronald was a conceited, spoilt, immature, young man, and I would not have got along with him.

Inter.:   Did you think that the dragon was rather foolish and simple-minded to fall for your tricks?

P.B.P.:   Oh yes, certainly, I think he also wanted to show off a bit. The ostentatious prig!!

Inter.:   The story goes that you didn't get married to Ronald after all. Have you anybody in mind?

P.B.P.:   I met him coming back from saving Ronald (groan). He took in my situation at once, and bought me my choice of clothes. We'll be getting married in the Spring.

Inter.:   Well, I'm afraid that we must conclude this interview, and I am sure that you will join me in all the best wishes for the Paper Bag Princess.

Some teachers and children might like to tape the interview. However, I normally find this is not necessary.

When sufficient time has been allowed, the group re-forms and the pairs present their interviews, one taking the role of the interviewer, the other the character.

Variations to this strategy

One possible variation to this strategy is to vary the interviewer's identity and role. The students could be asked to act as TV reporters, chat show hosts, radio news interviewers, etc. They can also be asked to conduct a panel discussion involving several characters and a few 'experts' who might have something relevant to add concerning a special problem. For example, a panel discussion could be set up that includes the BFG, Sophie, the chief of police and the Queen's special secretary on 'social matters'. This panel might then discuss the terrible problem of the giants who continue to eat innocent children (see *The BFG*, Dahl, 1982).

Literary sociogram

Introduction

This technique was first developed by Johnson and Louis (1985). It requires the reader to construct a sociogram depicting all the characters in a story and the interrelationships between them. The great advantage of sociograms, is that just by completing one the reader comes to appreciate and understand the text more. The reader is required to reflect upon the personality of each character, the complex interplay between the characters, and the subtleties of meaning often overlooked with a single superficial reading of text.

Procedure

The sociogram is produced by writing each character's name within a circle, and then representing the interactions between them using lines. The nature of the interaction is indicated by writing several words which briefly summarize this relationship. Each encounter with another character is represented briefly across the line linking them, with a comma separating each separate interaction (see Fig. 6.4).

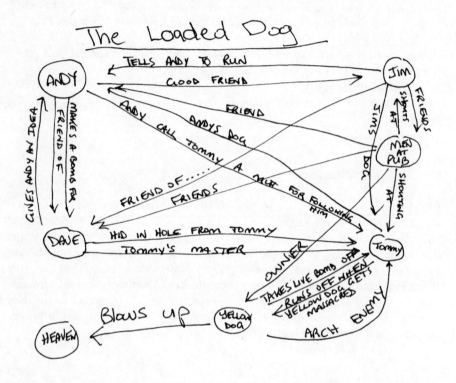

Fig. 6.4   A literary sociogram for the story *The Loaded Dog* (Lawson, 1970), drawn by Scott aged 11.

This is not an easy technique and it requires a careful introduction. It is necessary for the teacher to demonstrate the construction of a sociogram for a text that has already been shared with the class. A text with a manageable number of characters should be chosen. The first attempt at this should be simple enough to be completed quickly, so that the class can see how it works at the story level. The process should be started by asking the class to brainstorm a complete list of characters from the story. Once this has been done, the teacher selects the central character and begins the sociogram, adding less important characters in turn and representing the relationship between each using lines and comments.

It will probably be necessary to demonstrate at least two sociograms, although it is possible to get the children involved quickly after the first attempt by asking them to suggest characters and interactions. The teacher will need constantly to erase parts of the sociogram as it builds up, moving characters to accommodate extra interactions, and so on. It should be stressed to the children that several drafts of each sociogram can be completed. However, it should be pointed out that it is not necessary for the sociogram to be neat, as long as it can be used to discuss the text.

Although children can complete sociograms individually, I prefer it to be a group activity. The great advantage with group work is that there is a greater amount of knowledge that can be shared and more personal insights concerning the characters. Finally, it should be remembered that the product of this strategy is not important, it is the process involved and the insights gained that really matter.

Variations to this strategy

There are many simple variations to this strategy. For example, one could complete several sociograms for the one book at different key points in the plot. In this way, it is possible to compare the changing relationships as the story progresses. Other variations can be made in the procedures, e.g. one might ask students to complete them in small groups and then compare their products, or, alternatively, individuals might like to complete their own sociogram for a book they have been reading.

A final word

The strategies outlined above show that there is an alternative to traditional comprehension instruction. Although these activities are all different, they share many common features:

1. They help readers to create meaning as they encounter texts.
2. They require readers to construct a coherent understanding of whole texts.
3. They encourage excursions into other forms of meaning-making (such as writing, drawing, dramatization, etc.) to create a more complete understanding of the text that is read.
4. The teacher is vitally involved as a facilitator, modelling and demonstrating strategies that effective readers use to make sense of texts.

The ideas offered are not meant to be exhaustive. Rather, they are meant to act as examples of the types of strategies that can be planned for literary texts. The way teachers use the above ideas, and the alternative strategies that teachers themselves develop, will vary depending upon the text being read, the students being taught, and the context within which the lesson takes place. It is important that this is the case. The ideas outlined must never become activities that are ends in themselves. The focus must always be upon the book, not the strategies that the teacher is using to help the students get inside the book. I will expand on this theme in Chapter 10, which attempts to show how ideas like the above can be used in an integrated way, rather than as separate activities.

CHAPTER 7

Strategies for developing the comprehension of factual texts

Chapter 6 was concerned with strategies that assist the comprehension of literary texts. This chapter is concerned with factual texts. As outlined in Chapter 2, reading purpose and text genre (interrelated concepts) have a profound effect upon the way we read. If a book which is written in report-form on life in Africa is read to find out facts about the lifestyle of the Bushmen of the Kalahari, then it will most likely be read 'efferently' (to use Rosenblatt's term), because the reader tries to ascertain what it is that the author has attempted to convey about these people. While it is possible to read such a text 'aesthetically', it will defeat the object of gathering information about the Kalahari Bushmen.

One of the problems I have found as a teacher, is that many students have problems reading to find information, formulate an argument, ascertain an author's point of view, determine bias, summarize content, and so on. This chapter contains strategies which I have found help students to read for these and other purposes.

Semantic outlines

Introduction

This strategy requires readers to create a semantic outline which summarizes a factual text. Just as readers often have trouble constructing a coherent understanding of narrative texts, they often have difficulty understanding factual texts. This technique helps to show children that factual texts are quite different from narrative texts. Furthermore, it provides a means to help them construct a coherent understanding of the text, rather than a set of unrelated facts. Any teacher who has asked children to summarize a text, will know just how difficult children find it working with factual texts. The strategy that is outlined is of particular use when summarizing reports.

Procedure

To use this strategy, the teacher will need first to select a text from a social studies or science book, an encyclopaedia, or even a reading laboratory card (the texts can be used and the questions discarded). In the initial modelling lessons, the teacher chooses the text. However, after the class has been taken through the process several times, they should apply it to texts they have chosen themselves.

I start by telling the group that they are going to read an extract to see what they can learn about the topic, and stress that once they have read it they will have to organize and record new information in a form they can remember later and use to share with others. After these preliminary comments, I read the text to them. Once it is read, I ask them what they think the main idea of the extract is, and ask them to write it down. We then discuss the alternatives and write them on the blackboard or overhead projector. Usually, students suggest a variety of main ideas, ranging from unrelated statements to minor specific details. For example, one group I worked with suggested the following main ideas for a text entitled 'Raising the Titanic' (Education Department of Victoria, 1980):

The Titanic	Wreck of Titanic
The sinking of the Titanic	Raising the Titanic
Why the Titanic sank	Dangers of icebergs
The ship contained a fortune in jewels	The ship hit an iceberg

Once I have written the students' suggestions on the board or overhead projector, I choose one of these topics (attempting to reach some kind of consensus). Next, I ask the group to suggest ideas from the text that tell them something about the topic. Once again, some of these are shared in a brief brainstorming session and are written on an overhead projector or blackboard.

The next step is to show the group that the information they have collected needs to be organized in some form. The information the group has suggested (and which is recorded) is then used to demonstrate this process. I then explain that this can be done in a variety of ways. For example, using numbers to mark each point in a specific category, using colour-coding or some other graphic code (e.g. crosses, asterisks, etc.) – in fact, any form that makes sense to them. Figure 7.1 is the outcome of a group-sharing session based on the text 'Raising the Titanic'.

The first lesson of this type may end here. The next lesson may then involve a repetition of the previous lesson with a different text (this might be done a number of times), or you might proceed to the next stage.

The point of this type of lesson is to organize information, and therefore I usually demonstrate different formats, including sample lists, skeletal outlines, semantic webs, etc. At this stage I then try to construct one on an

What was the main idea: THE TITANIC WAS SO
SUPPOSED TO BE UNSINKABLE

List all the important details which tell us more about this idea:

(1) UNSINKABLE
(1) MAIDEN VOYAGE
(2) ONLY 705 PEOPLE LIVED
(2) NOT ENOUGH LIFE BOATS
(3) IT LIES 3½ KM DOWN ON OCEAN UNDER WATER FLOOR
(2) THE CARPATHIA WAS THE FIRST RESCUE SHIP THERE
(3) EXPERTS BELIEVE THE TITANIC IS WORTH $250 MILLION
(2)(3) IT SANK ON THE 14TH APRIL 1912
(1) IT WAS CARRYING 2190

Fig. 7.1 The result of a group brainstorming session to organize the significant details for *Raising the Titanic* (Education Department of Victoria, 1980).

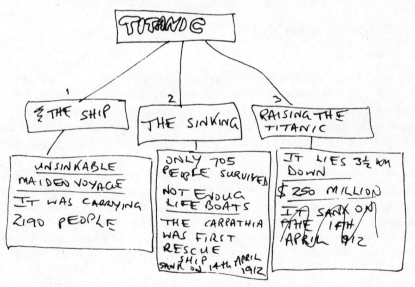

Fig. 7.2 One child's semantic web for *Raising the Titanic* (Education Department of Victoria, 1980).

overhead projector or blackboard, probing the class for more information as I go. It is important for the teacher to stress that it is his or her representation of the information, and that the children might organize it quite differently. The example shown in Fig. 7.2 shows how one child tried to organize his recall of the text 'Raising the Titanic' using a semantic web.

The final step in this lesson is to show students how their outline can be turned into a summary. To do this, I show and read a number of models, and then demonstrate how a summary should be written. As I have already indicated, the first attempt (or two) at this strategy might simply consist of a group discussion and some limited recording by individual children of the main topics and some supporting points. However, as the group grows in confidence, they should be encouraged to follow the process right the way through, culminating in their own representations of the information learned from reading the text.

Variations to this strategy

Within the above procedure, I have outlined many variations, e.g. the teacher can vary the number of new processes introduced in a single lesson, or the way in which processes are modelled. Also, the type of text shared will have a strong influence upon the task. While I prefer to start with simple reports, other text forms can be used. No two classes will have exactly the same needs in this area, and therefore variations to the above format are inevitable.

Talk-to-the-author sessions

Introduction

This is a strategy which is designed to help students engage with factual texts. Far too often children read factual texts at a surface level, failing to comprehend fully the author's intended meaning. As a result, the texts they construct as they read, often consist of a series of isolated details. Readers often fail to allow the text to challenge their thinking about the topic. Reading a text critically requires the reader to engage in dialogue with the text or the author. Talk-to-the-author is designed to move readers beyond the literal reading of factual texts and, in particular, to encourage them to differentiate between fact and opinion, and search for the author's biases, as well as his or her point of view. The strategy achieves this by encouraging readers to interact with the author as they read, by recording personal comments and questions in the margin.

Procedure

To use this strategy, a number of suitable texts will need to be prepared. They should be between 200 and 1000 words in length, and may be selected from magazines, newspapers, old reading laboratories, etc. Once the texts are chosen, I photocopy them, leaving a wide margin down one side of the page. Alternatively, the texts can be retyped.

Before asking my students to attempt this activity, I demonstrate it on the overhead projector (using a text that will not be used later). I explain to the group that the aim of the task is to read the text and make comments and ask questions as if interacting with the author. However, because the author is not available, I explain that these comments and questions need to be written alongside the text. I always point out that this helps me to appreciate the text more fully and come to a more thorough understanding of what it is trying to teach me.

Once the technique has been demonstrated, I ask my students to choose a text from several alternatives, which they then read, at the same time making comments and asking questions where they feel they are necessary (see Fig. 7.3). At first, students find this task difficult, but if they persist, the benefits are worth the extra effort.

Variations to this strategy

The format that this strategy takes can be easily varied. One variation involves altering the way in which the comments are written. For example, one might not photocopy a text, preferring instead that the children simply record their comments and questions on a sheet of paper. This tends to fragment the reading a little, but it does permit a greater variety of texts to be used – and with less preparation. A second variation concerns the way in which the strategy is applied. For example, pairs of children could read a text together, taking it in turns to read parts out loud. As they read, they can stop to make comments and both students can record them in the margin.

Estimate, read, respond, question (ERRQ)

Introduction

ERRQ is based upon a strategy first developed by Dorothy Watson (1985). It requires readers to actively engage with texts in order to link new information to background knowledge. It is a strategy that requires readers to engage in a recursive process of reading, writing and talking.

Procedure

To begin the lesson, I explain what ERRQ stands for and introduce the class to the process by demonstrating it on an overhead projector, using a short, single-page text divided into several sub-sections. This usually has at least one piece of illustrative material.

I then begin to go through each of the steps – I explain that I have scanned the text already (the starting point for this strategy) by looking at the sub-headings, illustrations and diagrams, and reading the first few sentences

NED KELLY

where did he go?

On his release, he stayed out of trouble for more than two years, working as a timber cutter and station hand. At the age of twenty-two he went prospecting for gold. When the squatters in the area reported horses and cattle missing, the police suspected Ned. However, they could not prove that he had anything to do with the losses.

Can you be arrested for being drunk?

Ned was arrested soon after in Benalla for being drunk. When he was taken to court the next day a fight broke out between Ned and the four policemen who were escorting him. A Justice of the Peace stopped the fight and during the following trial told the magistrate that the police had caused the fight. Ned was fined for being drunk the night before and had to pay for the damage to police uniforms.

In April 1878, seven months after the Benalla arrest, one of the policemen in the fight, Constable Fitzpatrick, went to the Kelly homestead at Greta to investigate horse stealing. The constable claimed that at the homestead he was shot at by Ned Kelly, bashed by Mrs Kelly, and had his gun stolen by Ned's brother, Dan, while two neighbors watched. The Kellys argued that Fitzpatrick was drunk and to blame for the incident. They stated that Ned wasn't even there and hadn't been home for three weeks.

where was he?

MRS KELLY ARRESTED

Mrs Kelly and the two neighbors were arrested. Warrants were issued for the arrest of

Why?

Ned and Dan Kelly. Ned was furious that his mother had been arrested, and he and Dan offered to give themselves up if his mother and the two neighbors were released. The police refused the offer. At the trial Mrs Kelly and the neighbors were given gaol sentences.

Why?

WANTED

Ned and Dan were joined in hiding in the bush by two friends, Steve Hart and Joe Byrne. The police sent a party of four policemen to capture them. But the Kellys found the police first, at Stringybark Creek. After a shoot-out, three of the policemen were dead. *Where's that?*

The Stringybark Creek massacre, as it was called in the press, was the beginning of the "Kelly outbreak". Newspapers in the colony of Victoria were full of reports of the Kelly gang. They had been declared outlaws by the government, which meant that anyone could shoot them on sight. *wheres that?*

The gang robbed the bank at Euroa and in New South Wales took over the town of Jerilderie. There, the gang took the police by surprise and paraded up the main street disguised in police uniforms. Ned wanted to find the local newspaper editor. Ned had written a letter defending himself and wanted it printed. But the editor had earlier written a story about "the cowardly murders at Stringybark Creek". He was afraid that Kelly might have seen the story, so he left his office and hid in a creek until the gang left town.

BIG WITHDRAWAL

A local schoolteacher was going into the Jerilderie bank as the gang was walking out, loaded with the bank's cash. Ned asked him what he wanted. The teacher replied that he had come to make a withdrawal.

"You're too late. Ned Kelly has withdrawn it all," laughed Ned.

Authorities in New South Wales and Victoria were outraged by the Kelly gang. A reward of £8000 was offered, for the capture of the outlaws. This was a huge reward for the time. *What is that in dollars?*   (Continued next page.)

Fig. 7.3   A sample of one child's first attempt at a talk-to-the-author session with *Ned Kelly* (Carroll, 1980).

of several sections. I point out that we are now going to *estimate* what the text is about. I show them the first page of the text and tell them what I think it is about. These brief comments are written in note form on the top of the first page.

Next, I explain that it is important to read the whole text right through. This is done by reading it aloud to the group, pointing out that they would normally read the text silently if working alone. Before starting, I stress that as the text is read it is important to think of ideas it triggers, previous texts that have been read or seen (e.g. TV documentaries), images that come to mind, ideas they find hard to understand or agree with, and so on.

After reading the text, I explain that it is then useful to respond to it in some way. This is an opportunity to share the thoughts that the reader has had during reading. I share some of my own thoughts and explain that if there is no-one to share these ideas with, it is useful to write them down. In this way they can be shared with someone else later, or simply re-read to reflect upon one's reading.

Finally, I suggest that this type of response should be followed by some self-questioning. Usually, the reader asks him or herself several questions about the content of the text. For example, what was it about? What was its 'big idea'? What am I still puzzled about? What do I have trouble accepting?

Variations to this strategy

There are many variations to this strategy. For example, it can be used with narrative texts, which requires some changes to the procedures. However, variations for factual texts include having students work in pairs, working individually on the same text as a group and sharing after 'estimating', 'responding' as a group, and pooling questions.

Retelling

Introduction

Retelling is basically a strategy designed to encourage students to recall a text that they have read. Its usefulness as a comprehension strategy has been well documented (see, e.g. Brown and Cambourne, 1987), because the retelling of a text forces the reader to 'revisit' the text they have constructed in memory, which in turn helps them to construct a more coherent representation of what they have read.

Procedure

As with all of the strategies in this chapter, it is important to demonstrate it to the class. Using an overhead projector, I show the children a short factual text of approximately 500 words. It is important at the outset to establish the purpose of the reading (i.e. collect facts on a specific topic, test someone else's ideas etc.). Once this has been done, I explain to the class that before I read the text I try to predict what the piece might be about by using the title, sub-headings and any illustrative material. I share these predictions and then read the text aloud to the class, explaining that as I read I judge the accuracy of my predictions.

After the text has been read, I share my retelling with the class. This can be done either orally or in written form. It should be explained that the written form will vary depending upon the reader's purpose. For example, if I was searching for facts on a specific topic, my retelling would simply be in the form of a list. However, if my purpose was to summarize a description of a natural disaster, it would more likely be in prose form. It is important to stress that during this process one should not look back to the text – it should be re-told from memory.

Once the retelling is complete, the class can be asked to comment upon the accuracy of the retelling: how does it compare with the original text? By placing the text on the overhead projector, the class can make more informed comments.

Following the demonstration of the strategy, I start to involve my students more in the process. At first we share the same text, all reading silently at the same time and then retelling it verbally to a partner. Later, I ask them to undertake a written retelling, which is shared with someone else. This sharing allows the students to compare each other's texts to discern differences, inaccuracies, etc.

Variations to this strategy

There are many variations to this basic strategy (Brown and Cambourne, 1987, provide a more detailed discussion which most teachers will find useful), one of which relates to changes in text form. For example, a range of factual texts can be used (e.g. newspaper reports, editorials, procedural texts, etc.), as well as narrative texts. It is also useful to vary the procedures, e.g. the strategy might be conducted with small groups or in pairs. The texts can be read orally or silently, together or alone. The variations are endless.

Cloze procedures

Introduction

The cloze procedure was first used by journalists to test the readability of newspapers. Educators began using it to assess the readability of school reading materials. Later, teachers began to use it for instructional purposes (Hopkins, 1978), e.g. to encourage readers to make predictions as they read, for the priming of semantic and syntactic information (Cairney, 1983), and to help with the comprehension of cohesive ties triggered by text elements like pronouns (Chapman, 1979, 1983).

Although some writers are critical of cloze, it still appears to be useful when used with factual texts. It is included here because it is seen as a valuable way of heightening engagement with factual text, of encouraging students to read for deeper meaning.

Procedure

After selecting a suitable passage for demonstration purposes, 1 in 10 words is deleted. The simplest way of doing this is to delete them with correcting fluid. The only problem with this procedure, however, is that it leaves a space the size of the word, which acts as a visual cue, thus reducing the reader's dependence upon meaning-based cues. One way around this is to type the passage, leaving spaces that are of an equal length.

As I read the passage aloud, I share my predictions for the missing words and the reasoning behind them. Later, I involve the students in the process before finally allowing them to complete a passage individually.

Variations to this strategy

There are many variations to this strategy, based on text form, number of deletions, form of the deletion, and manner in which the text is read and the gaps filled. For example, 1 in 5 words could be deleted instead of 1 in 10. Content words (i.e. nouns, verbs, adjectives and adverbs) or structural words (i.e. conjunctions, pronouns, articles and prepositions) could be removed. The task can be undertaken individually, as a class, or in small groups, the latter providing group consensus in action as students decide which filler words are best.

Also, the words that have been deleted could be supplied to the students in the form of a jumbled list, or complete phrases could be removed. The latter has been referred to elsewhere as 'framing' (see Cairney, 1985b) and only requires the teacher to provide a text-level skeleton with large gaps.

Directed research/thinking

Introduction

This model is based upon a more detailed approach developed by Morris and

Stewart-Dore (1984), which they label 'Effective Reading in Content Areas' (ERICA). It is designed to help readers 'learn to learn from text', its primary purpose being to help students to learn how to find, read and use factual texts to complete a variety of written tasks.

Procedure

One way I use this strategy involves preparation for reading using structured overviews, directed reading of the text, reflection upon the text, selection and organization of information and, finally, the recording of ideas in written form. Each of these stages is demonstrated separately for the class a number of times before they are encouraged to use the model alone. However, to simplify the description, I will outline how the complete process is demonstrated.

I begin by selecting a text of approximately 500 words. Having told the class of my chosen topic (e.g. 'Ned Kelly'), I display my structured overview using an overhead projector (see Fig. 7.4). As I draw the overview, I tell the class its purpose is to help them organize the ideas within the text as it is read. This overview can be presented to the readers by the teacher, or it can be prepared by readers themselves (individually or in groups) using their existing knowledge before the passage is read. In both cases, the overview acts as an advance organizer; however, I prefer the latter because it encourages students from the outset to prime their existing knowledge as they approach a text.

Having completed my stuctured overview, I encourage each student to prepare his or her own for a text that we have already shared. They are then encouraged to share their overviews within small groups. The great advantage of this is that students are able to pool their collective wisdom before reading the text.

The next stage of the process is to guide their reading of the text. This can be done in a number of ways, but I prefer to use a variation of Stauffer's (1969) Directed Reading–Thinking Activity. Briefly, the teacher guides the reading of the text (either oral or silent) by asking specific questions at certain points; making statements about the content; directing attention to diagrams, pictures, graphs, etc.; referring back to the structured overview; and so on.

After the text is read in this way the students are given the opportunity to react to it or reflect upon its content in small groups. This discussion is often given focus by asking specific questions. For example: What was the text about? What did you learn for the first time? What was the text's 'big idea'?

The students are then asked to gather information and record it in some form that will aid their learning and recall of content, and permit them to share that content with others. A variety of note-making strategies can be introduced, although I regularly use outlining. A number of formats can be used, but when introducing this technique to students I usually provide a

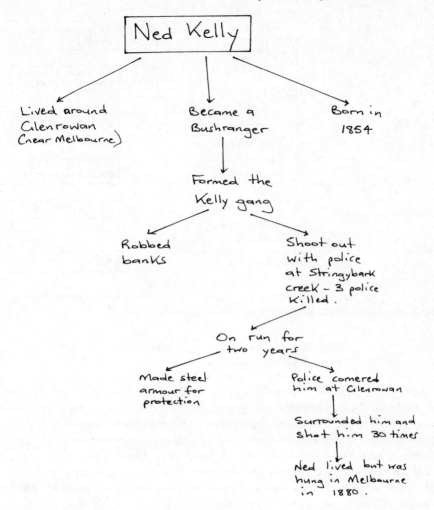

Fig. 7.4 A structured overview for a text about the Australian bush ranger *Ned Kelly* (Carroll, 1980).

simple frame (see Fig. 7.5) which requires the students to find the main idea(s), supporting ideas, and examples.

Once the students are content with their notes, all that remains to be done is to turn this into a written form that is appropriate for the purpose set. For example, if the purpose was to find out what a specific author has to say on a topic, then a summary would be most appropriate. Once again, it is important to demonstrate on the overhead projector how notes are turned into a summary.

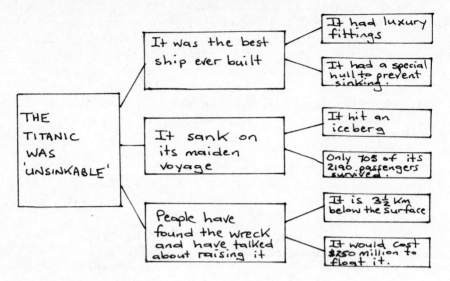

Fig. 7.5   An example of one student's use of the outlining technique for *Raising the Titanic* (Education Department of Victoria, 1980).

Variations to this strategy

There are several variations that can be made to this basic strategy. At every stage of the guided process changes can be made, e.g. structured overviews can be deleted and replaced by priming of the top-level structure (i.e. organizational frameworks that are used by authors to present content). Those top-level structures which are used frequently include comparison–contrast and cause-effect (see Morris and Stewart-Dore, 1984, for a more detailed discussion). The formats used to collect information and make notes can be varied, different methods can be used for outlining, and alternative formats for note making can be introduced. Finally, the manner in which the total strategy is introduced can vary depending upon the purpose of the reading and the level of ability of the students. It is important that the above discussion should act purely as a framework. Teachers should modify these procedures to suit the needs of their students.

Problem prowling

Introduction

Problem prowling is designed to be used with a variety of factual texts including encyclopaedias, directories and magazines. Its aim is to encourage students to read relevant sources to solve a problem, not simply summarize information. To do this, considerable use is made of group discussion and writing. The discussion of a focused question or problem acts as an advance organizer for reading, and has the effect of helping readers to focus their attention as they read in a far more disciplined way. This helps to avoid the tendency of students to read factual texts simply to summarize information, giving little thought for the original problem that was to be investigated.

Procedure

Having demonstrated problem prowling, the teacher should allow the students an opportunity to complete all stages of this specialized reading process.

The first step in the process is to identify a problem, usually in the form of a question. The students should begin to use this process for themselves in groups of 4–6, so that they can identify a problem of mutual interest. At times, it is useful to identify a broad area within which they might work (e.g. transport), but this is not necessary. Once the problems have been identified, the students are encouraged to make some predictions about them, i.e. to think about solutions to their problems and anticipate what the relevant reading sources might suggest. For example, one group came up with the following problem and predictions:

Problem: How do cars affect our environment?
- Cars kill lots of animal life
- Cars pollute the atmosphere
- Cars cause lots of problems because of their smell and noise
- Roads are ugly
- People dump old cars when they are no good any more

Once the students have met together as a group, I usually ask them to share their predictions about the problem with the class, one student acting as reporter for the group.

In a following lesson, students are encouraged to go to the library to find at least five books that would be of use when investigating their problem. Once again, the assumption is that students will have been given some instruction on the use of indexes and tables of contents. It is sometimes useful to provide a pro-forma so as to make the task easier, normally a sheet with the headings 'Author', 'Title', 'Dewey Number' and 'Page References'.

Next, the students are asked to read the relevant sections of the books they have chosen to test their original predictions, and then record facts that relate to their original predictions and, under a separate heading, other relevant information they did not consider. This stage of the process can be achieved in a number of ways. For example, each student can read one of the books, making notes where relevant. The group can then meet together to share their discoveries and record them on chart paper, thereby summarizing all relevant information.

After this, the students are encouraged to discuss their investigations with others, sharing not only the interesting discoveries, but also the problems experienced. One useful format for the reporting back session is to ask group leaders to share one problem (if there was one) and three interesting discoveries.

The final stage in the process is to encourage students to prepare a report of their findings. Before doing this, it is important that the teacher discusses the form the final written text will take, and provides an example of the text genre to be used. For example, it might be a report, an outline or a semantic web. The students are then given the opportunity to complete their final written text, which is then shared and displayed.

Variations to this strategy

Some of the variations are simply minor changes to the procedures within each stage, whereas others may involve using more restricted problems that require special types of written reference material. For example, the students might decide to investigate a problem related to current affairs and which requires newspapers to be their primary source. Also the problem may require the use of more than one type of source material. For example, students attempting the problem 'How would I plan a holiday for my family to the United States of America?', would need to use maps, accommodation directories, travel brochures, airline timetables, holiday guides, etc. To make this task even more interesting, the teacher could specify a few parameters, e.g. two adults and two children will make the trip, £7000 spending money is available, the aim is to spend 21 days away. For a problem of this type, the same sequence of steps applies. However, the nature of the predictions at the beginning of the process will be slightly different. The following is one student's predictions to a problem having been given a number of parameters:

Problem: Plan a trip to the USA to the value of no more than £7000.

Student predictions
- I think I would visit Disneyland, Washington (to see the White House), New York, San Francisco, Los Angeles, Texas, the Grand Canyon, and Indianapolis to see the Indy 500.
- I will fly British Airways.
- In America I will travel by train from city to city.
- I think I will stay in hotels or guest houses.
- We will need to allow money for food and souvenirs.

Other problems would impose their own special demands and require the use of uniquely different reading materials, and once again different predictions. The following problems are typical of the variety that might be pursued:

- You have £8000 to furnish a new house. It has three bedrooms, a lounge, family room, bathroom and laundry. What furniture would you buy for a family of two adults and three children?
- Find out the history of the site that the school occupies. What was on this site before the school? How long is the recorded history of this place and what happened here?
- What are the special features of the armadillo?

Procedural project puzzlers

Introduction

This strategy is designed specifically for the reading of procedural texts, i.e. those which attempt to provide the reader with a set of instructions or steps to perform some task or solve a problem. Students meet texts of this type quite frequently (e.g. game instructions, instructions for building a model, procedures for using a piece of electrical equipment), and will do so even more often in later life. It is important to help them deal with texts of this type. This strategy is designed to engage readers in procedural texts so that the task to which the text refers can be completed satisfactorily.

Procedure

The procedural project puzzlers which follow are quite diverse in their requirements. However, each has a number of common elements: (1) they all require students to complete a specific task; (2) each strategy employs writing and drawing as well as reading; (3) students collaborate on each task. Possible procedural project puzzlers might include:

- Teach a game to another group of students by writing a simpler version of the rules provided.
- Complete a procedural task (e.g. build a model) and write an account of the directions that were followed. Use illustrations and diagrams to make the explanation clearer.
- Unscramble a set of instructions for either a piece of electrical equipment, a game, a recipe or a toy.

While each of these tasks is quite different, the procedures to be followed for each are similar. First, a number of different procedural texts should have been discussed with the students and the essential characteristics of the text specified. A 'games day' is one way of introducing this stage in the process.

The students bring games of their choice to school, which they then share with those students who have not played them before. In groups of 2-4, they are then encouraged to work out how each game is played. At the end of approximately 30 minutes, specific games are discussed and their instructions and rules are examined.

Once the students have become familiar with the basic features of a procedural text and have had the opportunity to read one in a situation like the games afternoon, it is time to look more closely at the reading and comprehension of a range of these texts. The second step in the process is usually a guided reading of a specific procedural text. Typically, students are given a common procedural text which they are to follow in groups of 2-3: recipes or craft instructions are good texts to use. The text is usually read one section at a time, with the students attempting to complete each step together. As each step is completed, the groups compare their progress: problems are discussed and then the next part of the text is read. The lesson continues in this way until the whole text has been read.

This step is usually repeated several times with different texts before the students embark on stage 3 of the process, which involves more independent work. The students are asked to read a text and show their understanding of it by transforming it into another text form. This might be their simplified version of a set of instructions, or a sequence of diagrams designed to make the completion of a task easier. The latter might be completed for texts which describe the construction of models, the use of a piece of equipment (e.g. bicycle pump) or recipes. The culmination of stage 3 is always the sharing of each group's work and the problems encountered.

Variations to this strategy

As the above procedure indicates, there are many possible variations, the majority of which are introduced by varying the types of text. Every effort should be made to do this. At times, theme sessions might be planned, where all the texts used are of a specific type, e.g: the instructions for craft activities, model construction, following directions found in a hardware shop, games, scavenger hunts, etc.

Editorial arguments

Introduction

The purpose of editorial arguments is to encourage students to read newspapers critically. Many students are passive readers and fail to realize that just because something appears in print, they are not compelled to agree with it. This strategy aims to encourage readers to engage with the text and make judgements about the perceived truth or logic of the author's arguments.

Procedure

This strategy should be used several times as a class before allowing students to attempt it alone. The teacher should make multiple copies of an editorial from a newspaper or magazine, or, alternatively, an overhead transparency so that the class can read along. The editorial selected should present a clear point of view. Before reading the text, I point out that editorials of this kind always express the views of the author and that readers are not compelled to agree with the arguments. In fact, I point out that many readers will inevitably disagree with all or part of the writer's arguments.

The teacher should then ask the class to underline the things with which they agree and to circle those with which they disagree as the teacher reads the text. After it has been read, the class can then share the things with which they agree with the arguments. In fact, I point out that many readers will inevitably disagree with all or part of the writer's arguments.

Once this has been done, the students should then read the text silently, again underlining the things with which they agree, but using a different coloured pen or pencil. They are then able to share any changes in their point of view, indicating why they think they may have done so.

When this process has been completed a number of times, the students can be asked to apply the strategy alone or in groups of 2–4.

Variations to this strategy

The procedures used can easily be varied by changing the format of the shared reading (e.g. as a class or in groups), the manner in which opinions are recorded (e.g. underlining, listing points of agreement on a separate sheet, etc.) and the type of text (e.g. letter to the editor, editorial, feature article, etc.). Other variations include providing several articles from different newspapers on the same topic, so that views can be compared, or collecting alternative views from several articles to mount a debate on the topic.

The strategy can also be modified to look at a different dimension of critical reading. For example, instead of reading to determine agreement/disagreement, readers could read critically to:

* discern bias;
* identify fact or opinion;
* determine substantiated or unsubstantiated arguments.

Schema prediction

Introduction

Schema prediction was designed to encourage students to activate relevant schemata (i.e. structures for organizing information held in memory) before reading a specific text. Readers develop a set of expectations about different text types based upon prior experiences they have had reading and writing texts of this type. Being able to activate relevant schemata enables the reader to organize information and understand the text more easily. This occurs because readers have a structure within which to fit information and, as a consequence, they have less demands placed upon their working memories. This allows greater memory capacity for the integration of information and the processing of text. As a result, this aids comprehension.

Procedure

This strategy is normally used a number of times as a whole class before asking students to apply it in groups or individually. To begin the process, the teacher should select a problem or question to be answered, e.g. 'What benefits to man are offered by the settlement of Antarctica?' The question should be both one of interest and relevance to the students. Once the problem is isolated, texts which seem to have some relevance to the topic are selected.

One text is selected and a relevant chapter is isolated, e.g. 'Antarctica: Wilderness or mineral resource?' The chapter heading is placed on the board and the students are asked to predict the content of that chapter. They are asked to list the possible sub-headings that will be used, and the maps, tables, figures and diagrams that might appear.

The class is then given the opportunity to skim through the chapter to look at the headings, sub-headings, diagrams, etc. In groups of 3–5 students, the results of this 'skim reading' are compared with their original predictions. What was consistent? What things surprised them?

After this discussion, the students (in the same groups) select a specific heading or sub-heading and predict 3–5 items that might appear in the section. The students then read the section individually to assess how close their predictions were to the text. They then re-form as a group and share their discoveries about the text.

This process can be repeated for other sections of the text, but should not be overdone. At the conclusion of the lesson, an attempt should be made to summarize the principle features of the text which has been read. In later lessons, comparisons should be drawn between the various texts that have been read: How do they differ in terms of language use, structure, formatting, style, diagramatic support material, and so on? The focus within each lesson should be upon the development and activation of text schemata that help to facilitate the comprehension of each text.

Variations to this strategy

There are a number of areas in which variations to this strategy can easily be made, e.g. the number of sections of text examined, the problem or question giving focus to the lesson, the grouping of students for discussion, etc. Also, there is a clear need to vary the type of text examined: each text type (e.g. historical account, geographical description, scientific report, etc.) has its own special features.

Conclusion

The above strategies are not meant to represent an exhaustive set. The aim has been to provide an indication of the diversity of strategies that can be used. All strategies conform to the principles outlined in previous chapters and are meant to serve as examples of the infinite possibilities for work with factual texts. The range of strategies that can be developed is limited only by one's imagination and resourcefulness.

CHAPTER 8

Whole-text strategies for younger readers

The purpose of this chapter is to outline a number of strategies that have proven effective for helping young students become literate. Each strategy has its own individual demands, but all share a number of common features:

1. They emphasize the reading of whole texts.
2. They involve considerable interaction, i.e. teacher–student and student–student.
3. They focus upon meaning.
4. They attempt to capitalize upon shared language experiences to enable students to achieve immediate success as meaning-makers.

I do not pretend that any of the techniques which follow are new. They are included here because they are consistent with the stated theoretical orientation to language, learning and teaching outlined in previous chapters. I hope that their description will encourage teachers to implement them.

Reading predictable books

Introduction

Predictable books are pieces of fiction which contain sufficient repetition in terms of content, rhyme and language patterns to enable students to anticipate what is coming next in the text. These books also have a good balance between written text and illustrations. Some examples of predictable books suitable for beginning readers are:

- *Are You My Mother?* by P.D. Eastman (1960)
- *The Very Hungry Caterpillar* by Eric Carle (1970)
- *A Fly Went By* by Mike McClintock (1958)
- *Mr Gumpy's Motor Car* by John Burningham (1973), and other Mr Gumpy books

- *The Best Nest* by P.D. Eastman (1968)
- *How Do I Eat It?* by Shigeo Watanabe (1979), and other books in this series of bear books.
- *Alexander and the Terrible, Horrible, No Good, Very Bad Day* by Judith Viorst (1973)
- *One Dragon's Dream* by Peter Pavey (1981)
- *Don't Forget the Bacon* by Pat Hutchins (1978)

Predictable books can be used the first day children attend school. At first, the teacher will select the books, but students will soon be able to make their own selections, both for reading independently and for sharing with other class members. The great strength of predictable books is that they enable teachers to share whole texts with students as soon as they begin school, they model the reading process, and they encourage students from their first encounter with print to read for meaning.

Procedure

The process of reading a predictable book usually begins with the teacher showing the cover and reading the title to the children (usually seated in a comfortable position in front of him or her on the floor). At this point, teachers frequently ask the children to indicate what they think the book is about. It is also sometimes useful to focus attention on the illustration on the cover. For example, when introducing *Don't Forget the Bacon* (Hutchins, 1978), a teacher could ask his or her pupils where they think the boy on the cover looks like he is going. The aim of this preliminary step is to prime relevant background knowledge, and to encourage the pupils to draw upon relevant schemata (structures for storing information in memory), so that predictions can be made about the story. However, it is important not to overdo this initial discussion.

After this short discussion, the story is usually read right through without interruption: I neither stop to offer explanations, nor do I actively seek to encourage the pupils to read along. However, they are not discouraged if they do join in spontaneously.

Following the first reading, I normally read it again, encouraging the children to join in where they can predict the text, e.g. 'But don't forget the bacon!' This time I pause, and use exaggerated expressions to try to encourage the children to join in. If the text has been well chosen, most of the children will have become involved in it by the end of the second reading. This process is repeated a number of times across a period of perhaps a week, and then the book is made available for independent and small-group reading. Teachers can also encourage the children to become engaged by allowing them to dramatize the text and so support the reading. Later in the year, I usually go back to each story, allowing time for them to be read again both as a class and in groups.

Variations to this strategy

The main way of varying this exercise is to use a number of different texts. However, 'big books' (i.e. books with large print) can be used instead (see the next section).

Shared reading

Introduction

Shared reading is closely related to the use of predictable books, but permits students to actually see the print as the text is read. It can be accomplished in small groups, with partners or as a whole class. One of the most common forms is the use of 'big books'. This form of shared reading owes a great deal to Don Holdaway (1979). It is an adaptation of the reading of predictable books and conforms to the major principles upon which this strategy is based. However, it has the added advantage that it allows children to learn the basic concepts of print (e.g. left to right, top to bottom, sound-symbol match, etc.) naturally as part of the reading process. Originally, teachers had to produce their own large versions of predictable books; however, a large number of publishers (e.g. Scholastic) now produce 'big book' versions of many of their titles.

Procedure

As with predictable books, teachers usually select the text to be read in the early stages. The book is shown to the class and once again an attempt is made to engage the readers, prime relevant background knowledge and encourage prediction. The teacher then reads the story, pointing just ahead of the words in the text being read.

After the first reading, the book is discussed briefly, and the children are allowed time to offer their personal responses to the text. It is then read again, with the children being encouraged to join in.

On other occasions (perhaps daily over a week), the text is read again, slowly handing over responsibility for the total reading of the text. This can be done in a number of simple ways, e.g. the children can participate in page turning and print pointing. Later, a number of simple variations to the reading can be used, such as:

- allowing the boys to read one part and the girls another;
- allowing an individual child to read one part and the class the rest;
- asking different groups to read the text for specific characters;
- having one child narrate, with small groups of children taking the part of specific characters, and others doing the sound-effects.

As with predictable books, after the big book has been used for approximately one week, it becomes available for independent reading.

Written conversation

Introduction

Written conversation, as the name suggests, is simply a conversation between two people that requires a written dialogue. It is an extremely useful way to introduce young pupils to the reading and writing of text. Its great value is that it requires them simply to use their knowledge of spoken language to create written language. It has the added advantage that it is a far more engaging form of writing than most of those that can be used with young children. Once again, it encourages students to become engaged in the reading and writing processes as meaning-makers, not simply decoders of text and spellers of words.

Procedure

Written conversation in its simplest form requires students in pairs to engage in dialogue. The first writer makes a statement about him or herself, shares an interesting idea, asks a question, and so on. The second writer then responds in writing and shares something as well. This continues back and forth until either partner runs out of things to say or becomes bored with the process. For young students, 10–15 minutes of this is usually sufficient – any more will lead to boredom.

There are a few basic rules which are necessary for the pupils to observe:

1. They are not permitted to talk during the conversation. If they are unsure of their partner's text, they should ask clarifying questions in writing.
2. The children are encouraged to include interesting information about themselves.
3. They should attempt to think of things to say that their partners will find interesting.
4. Spelling is not of major importance. The teacher should tell them that if they are unsure of a word, they should attempt to write it the best way they can.

I always introduce written conversation by modelling it for my students. To do this, I write a statement on an overhead projector or on the blackboard and invite specific students to respond. The following is a written conversation typical of those used with 7-year-olds:

> **T.C.**: Today I'm going to show you how to talk to each other using only writing. On my way to school today I saw a Wombat that had been run over. It always makes me sad to see dead animals along the road. What about you? Do you ever see dead animals on the road?
>
> **Kylie**: Onse I was cuming home from school and I saw a ded cat nr my conner and it was my frends cat.
>
> **T.C.**: Yes it's sad when someone has a pet killed. When I was about your age my cat Smokey was killed when my Dad stood on him. I carried him outside and put him on the grass but he was dead, his neck was broken.
>
> **Jason**: Me and Frank fown a derd fox in the boosh by the crik it wos al cuved in magets. . .

In this way, I manage to maintain a conversation with the class collectively. Written conversation should be used in this way two or three times before the children attempt it in pairs.

Because this is an informal, non-publishable form of writing, very young students can participate. Although 5-year-olds may use a number of invented spellings, they will still be able to communicate with their partners. As a general rule, children will be ready to commence written conversation when their knowledge of sound-symbol relationships has developed to the extent that they can write approximately half of the consonants and several vowels. At this stage, most writers will be attempting to write a variety of words and will have a store of perhaps 20–50 which they can both read and write.

Variations to this strategy

Most of the variations to this strategy involve changes to the procedures used to conduct the conversations. Some teachers may prefer to use more modelling before allowing their students to attempt their own conversations; others may prefer to use less. Students might also be allowed to conduct conversations in groups of 3–4 people, and they may be encouraged to conduct conversations with famous people or book characters. The latter is a wonderful way of encouraging children to 'get inside' the characters they meet in literature (see Chapter 6).

The language experience approach

Introduction

The language experience approach to early literacy development has been used in a variety of forms for decades. However, its use grew dramatically in the 1970s due to the work of Van Allen (1961). With the rise of 'process writing' methods, however, there has been a tendency to dismiss it as inappropriate because it wrests the control of writing away from the child. However, there still seems to be a place for it.

In essence, language experience involves encouraging students to dictate significant experiences they have had, so that the teacher can produce a written form of the student's spoken text. These experiences are identified and composed by the student, the teacher's job being simply to record faithfully what the student has said without changing the syntax or meaning. This is valuable because the texts that are produced reflect the student's experiences and language. This permits them to engage more readily with the text and read for meaning. Because content and language are familiar, students are able to use semantic and syntactic knowledge to supplement their knowledge of sound-symbol relationships, which are perhaps still developing. The end result is that the students are more able to read for meaning, and not simply attempt to decode print.

Procedure

The first point to stress is that language experience is not a substitute for the reading of literature and for students' writing their own texts. Language experience should be used alongside 'real' reading and writing. It is usually used with small groups of students or with individuals.

The first step when using language experience is to ask the students to share an experience that is significant to them, such as 'My dog Shep', 'The day I got lost', 'Rabbiting', 'My dad's metal detector', 'Football', and so on. Usually, language experience involves one child dictating his or her text to the teacher (or helper); however, it is possible for several children to compose a story together.

Normally, the text is written on a number of sheets of paper which will ultimately form a book. If the story is dictated by a young student, a single sentence may be recorded on each page. With older students, however, it is likely that the amount of text written on each page will be significantly longer.

When the text is completed, the teacher should read it back to the student(s) to make sure that it has been written down accurately. The students should then be encouraged to point out any errors. Once this has been done, the students are given the text and asked to illustrate each page.

Once the illustrations have been completed, the book is bound, a library card is inserted (to permit other students to borrow it) and it is presented to the student. After the teacher reads the book with its young author, he or she keeps it for at least a week. During this time, the text is read in a variety of ways and for a variety of purposes, e.g. to the class, to a partner, silently, to parents or friends, etc.

Finally, the book is placed in the class library so that it can be read by the other students. At a later date, I encourage my students to re-read their book and share it with others.

Variations to this strategy

There are many possible variations to this strategy, e.g. completing the dictated text as a group rather than individually, attempting to encourage students to dictate a range of text types (e.g. recipes, descriptions, poems, riddles, jokes, stories, instructions, messages), and simply varying the manner in which the text is presented (e.g. booklet form, wall chart, shape book, etc.).

Message board

Introduction

The message board is a valuable way to engage students in a social interaction process which is dependent upon written language. It involves the sharing of messages between class members. Some classes achieve this by providing a board on to which students pin notes (folded or in envelopes), with the name of the person to whom it is being sent clearly labelled. Others use a more sophisticated system which uses a set of alphabetized pigeon holes.

The message board is invaluable as a vehicle for early literacy development, and is a vital means for communication between all members of the group.

Procedure

Starting up a message board is fairly simple. After the board has been erected and suitably labelled, the process can be begun by writing a short message to each child. If the messages are pinned to the board before the start of a school day, it is fun for the children to discover the board and then realize that there is a message for each of them.

Once all of the students have discovered that there is a message for them, and they have had time enough to read it, the teacher should explain the reason for the message board. I normally inform my students that the board has been introduced so that we can:

* remind each other about upcoming events;
* tell other people about important things that have happened in our lives;
* share important class news;
* keep in touch with each other; and
* encourage each other by offering praise and feedback.

I then encourage the class to start communicating with each other. Although I continue to write to the pupils, I do this selectively, taking great care to make sure that someone is not forgotten and that I reply to all messages sent to me. I do, however, sometimes deliver a common message in the form of a memo:

STOP PRESS

I've got some GOOD news and BAD news for you.

First the bad news – we will not be having P.E. today because it is too wet.

The good news is that we will be having COOKING instead. How good are you at tossing pancakes? What about eating them?

Bye,

Mr C.

Once the message board has been started it is self-generating: students soon begin to communicate with each other about a wide range of topics and interests.

Variations to this strategy

Although it is possible to make minor changes to the above procedures, few are necessary. It is possible, however, to make changes to the network used for communication, e.g. setting up a message board that operates between classes. Also, a computer version of the message board could be used using one of the many communications links now available. This technology even makes it possible to communicate with students in other countries. A number of teachers have already discovered how exciting space-age communication can be.

Rhyme and rhythm in reading

Introduction

Children have a natural fascination for rhyme and rhythm. It is a very rare child who cannot think of some way to finish the following sentence:

Sticks and stones will break my bones but names will ____ ____ ____.

Chants and rhymes are a natural part of playground games. Children chant as they skip rope, recite rhymes for fun, and adopt well-known musical rhymes:

Found a peanut, found a peanut, found a peanut just now, where'd you find it, where'd you find it, where'd you find it just now, it was crunchy, hardly lumpy, on the benches it did lay . . .

With so much interest in rhyme and rhythm, it makes good sense to capitalize on this enthusiasm by translating well-known chants into print. This enables young students to read a well-known chant with little decoding skill and provides a confidence-boosting and enjoyable way to commence reading.

Procedure

There are many ways in which rhyme and rhythm can be used in early reading. The following represent several simple procedures.

1. *Chant shuffle.* This requires the teacher to write a well-known chant or rhyme on a piece of cardboard. Once this is done, it is introduced to the class and read out loud. If the text chosen is indeed a well-known one, then the students will probably join in before the teacher can finish. The text is used regularly over a period of a week following these simple procedures:

- As it is read the teacher should point to each word.
- The students should be encouraged to predict what comes next, by the teacher remaining silent for specific words or phrases.
- The students should be allowed to take turns pointing to the words.
- The reading patterns should be varied by allowing individuals and specific groups to take parts of the reading.

Once students are familiar with the text, the next stage involves cutting it into separate lines. These are jumbled up and distributed to the class. The teacher then asks the students who has the first line. Once this has been identified, it is placed on the board (using tape or pins) and the next line is requested. In this way the class reconstructs the complete text. Later, groups of students should be given the opportunity to complete the text themselves.

The final stage is to cut each line up into separate words. The words are distributed and each line reconstructed by asking 'Who has the first word?', 'Who has the next?', and so on.

2. *Innovating rhyming texts.* This simple and enjoyable variation requires the teacher to select a well-known rhyme or chant and to write part of it on the board or on the overhead projector. For example:

> Little Jack Horner sat in a corner,
> Eating his Christmas Pie,
> He put in his thumb,
> And pulled out a _____ .
> And _____ .

Before looking at the written version of the rhyme, it is recited from memory. Once this has been done, the class should be shown the partially completed version and encouraged to complete it with their own adaptation of the text. Before completing the rhyme, the class as a whole should select the words which they feel are most effective. For example:

Little Jack Horner sat in a corner,
Eating his Christmas Pie,
He put in his thumb,
And pulled out a GUN,
And SHOT MISS MUFFET FAIR IN THE EYE.

This new version of the rhyme is then read and kept for re-reading on future occasions.

3. *Using music with rhymes.* Skipping rhymes are one source of musical text that can be used for reading. However, there are many common examples that can be sung, not just from memory, but by reading the words. Rhyming songs like 'Found a Peanut', 'Sing a Song of Sixpence' and 'Hickory Dickory Dock' are enjoyable ways to introduce the class to the 'reading' of music.

Once several have been introduced and sung, it is even possible to adapt the musical text.

4. *Transforming well-known songs.* This is very similar to adapting chants. However, here the class tranforms well-known songs into funny renditions that can be sung using a printed version of the song produced by the class. For example, 'Jingle Bells' might be transformed in the following way:

Jingle bells, jingle bells,
Jingle all the way,
Oh what a pain it is to hear,
Those sleigh bells half the day . . .

The object behind this is to use existing, well-known rhythms and music, but to create a new text which will require students to attend more closely to the print.

Variations to this strategy

The above examples show that there are many ways to use rhyme and rhythm for early reading. The examples given are hardly exhaustive. Variations to the above are limited only by one's ingenuity and stock of well-known rhymes, chants, songs and riddles. Teachers will find that the primary source of material for this strategy is the children themselves. Even very young children will be able to contribute texts of this type for early reading.

CHAPTER 9

Getting it all together: Integrating the reading and writing of factual texts

The purpose of this chapter is to outline an approach that can be used for integrating the reading and writing of factual texts. As a teacher, I have been constantly frustrated by my students' inability to write reports, or even just summarize factual texts. In my first years of teaching, I constantly set projects only to find that my students' efforts were very poor. For example, if I asked 12-year-olds to 'Do a project on China', they typically looked for one encyclopaedia or book with information on China, and indiscriminately copied out great slabs of information.

After some time, I began to question my own practices. When I said 'Do a project', what did I expect? What type of written text did I expect them to produce? Was I expecting them to write a report, a piece of exposition, an outline? What were my students' expectations of 'doing projects'? I began to observe my students and noticed that when asked to complete a project a common pattern emerged:

1. First, they spent a large amount of time planning and drawing a title page.
2. They then began to plan the format for the presentation of their work – the number of pages, where the illustrations would go, what type of borders would be used, how the headings would be written, and so on.
3. A search would then be made for suitable pictures in old travel magazines, newspapers and brochures.
4. The project layout would be completed, pictures would be cut out and pasted in the preferred place in the project book, and the odd picture copied or traced.
5. A search would begin for a book that mentioned the topic. Often be-leaguered and somewhat frustrated, the children's parents would do most of this searching for them in public libraries.
6. Finally, the finishing touches would be made to the presentation of the project – sub-headings finished, borders completed, etc.

As I reflected upon this common pattern, it became apparent that my students were more concerned about how their projects looked rather than what they contained. I realized that I had been inadvertently contributing to this attitude by commenting mainly upon the appearance of their completed work and failing to specify the written form expected. Also, I was not helping them to develop the necessary research strategies that would enable them to become effective readers and writers of factual texts.

Examining my assumptions about project work

This critical incident in my teaching career made me more aware of the help my students needed if they were to become effective users of factual texts. When I had asked my students to 'Do a project on China', I had assumed that they were able to:

- locate suitable source books relevant to a topic;
- use a wide range of reading strategies to search for relevant information;
- extract information from a variety of sources using a table of contents and an index;
- record relevant information in some form, e.g. notes, outline, etc.;
- translate rough notes into an appropriate text form, e.g. a report;
- produce illustrations, maps, diagrams and tables to support their texts; and
- maintain a strong commitment to a topic which was not of their own choosing.

When I realized that these assumptions were incorrect, I set about helping my students to become more proficient readers and writers of factual texts. My first attempts largely involved the use of learning activities that required them to engage with factual texts for some specific purpose, e.g. I would give my students the name of a book and ask them to find three others in the library covering a similar topic (see Cairney, 1983). While these activities provided some help in specific location and study skills, I found that my students still had difficulty integrating the various strategies necessary for completing a project.

I began experimenting with integrated approaches that required the students to select a topic for research and to apply a wide range of reading and writing strategies. The following description of an integrated approach to the reading and writing of factual texts has proved to be very effective at improving students' competence.

Helping students to become researchers

This approach to factual reading and writing requires a number of sequenced lessons. It is not a quick and easy method for turning students into researchers – there is no such method. However, it is an effective way of engaging students more purposefully in the reading of factual texts, thus leading to the production of a variety of written text forms. The overall approach owes much to the classroom-based work of two former colleagues, Paul Williams and Ann Pulvertaft.

I should stress that the sequence of lessons that follows (see Table 9.1) is varied in accordance with the abilities, age and prior reading and writing experiences of the students. The sequence outlined is one of many that could be followed and has been used with 11-year-olds.

Table 9.1 Summary of the research writing process

Step 1	Outline intention of doing research; set broad topic area; model brainstorming; ask students to brainstorm own topic
Step 2	Model discovery draft and ask students to attempt their own
Step 3	Discuss the text genre to be used (e.g. report) and outline the sub-headings to be used to organize information. Model the procedure to be used to categorize information using own discovery draft
Step 4	Discuss note-making skills and formats and demonstrate basic techniques for the class. Discuss the location skills necessary to find information and take students to the library to obtain information on topics
Step 5	Demonstrate methods for reorganizing notes in order to produce cohesive texts. Ask students to reorganize their notes and attempt a draft of one section
Step 6	All students complete the draft of their reports
Step 7	Provide opportunities for the revision and proof-reading of drafts
Step 8	Discuss the use of illustrative material and presentation formats. Show some finished reports. Allow students to begin to plan a format for presentation
Step 9	Approve each student's format for the report and allow him or her to complete the work
Step 10	Share the reports and display them for others to read

The first lesson begins with the teacher announcing that the students are to learn how to become researchers. I ask them to comment upon their previous experience with project work and, if necessary, raise a number of problems that I have observed with work of this kind. I usually show the class a completed project (from another class group) that contains sections of information simply copied from a source book, reflecting little understanding of the task. I then show them another one that is substantially the students' work. The two are compared and then I tell them that I am going to help them conduct research work that leads to written reports that indicate their learning.

Next, I provide the class with a number of subjects for possible research (e.g. transportation, animals, countries of the world, etc.) and ask their opinions about each. After each option has been explored, one is chosen for further study. At this stage of the lesson, I suggest that it is necessary to brainstorm a suitable topic from within this broad subject area. Before asking my students to do this, I first demonstrate how it is done. This procedure is followed throughout the sequence of lessons, by modelling the techniques on the blackboard or overhead projector.

I begin brainstorming topics, commenting on each as I go: Why did I think of this one? Would it be interesting? Would others want to read about it? Do I know much about the topic? I end the demonstration by selecting a topic and explaining why it has been chosen (see the result of such a modelling session in Fig. 9.1). I then ask the students to brainstorm their topics and discuss them with a partner before finally deciding which topic is to be researched.

Figure 9.1 The result of the modelling of topic brainstorming for a group of students aged 10 years.

I commence the second lesson by reminding the class of the topic I had chosen in the brainstorming session. I then explain that I need to compile a discovery draft, which involves writing down everything that I already know about the topic. I tell them that it should be done quickly, so that their ideas flow freely. As I write, I make the occasional comment if I am unsure about the accuracy of my statements (e.g. 'I think they're mainly brown'). I then ask the students to complete their own discovery drafts, after which they can be read to a partner. A class discussion is then held to discover what is already known about the topic – 'How much do I already know?' 'What do I need to find out?'

In the third lesson, I point out that we need to continue our research, and eventually present our learning in report form (see Collerson, 1988). It is important to stress that a report is just one genre that can be used. However, because of its simplicity, it is a good starting point when introducing this integrated approach. I then read out several reports, pointing out their major features, i.e. they usually commence with a general classification that defines the topic of the report to a wider body of knowledge (e.g. 'Snakes are Reptiles'). This is followed by a series of details about the topic, categorized in some way. We then discuss the likely categories of information that can be used for the topic in question, which will effectively become the sub-headings within the report. These need to be sufficiently generic to match each child's topic. The students eventually determine their own categories.

Once again I show the class my discovery draft and suggest that the information can be categorized under the headings outlined. This is done using one of several strategies, e.g. colour coding, a numbering system, etc. (see Fig. 9.2).

After asking the students to comment on whether or not my draft is deficient in some way, I tell them that I need further information. I stress that it may be necessary to test the accuracy of the information in the discovery draft as the research is conducted. The students then examine their own discovery drafts, code them, and discuss any deficiencies with a partner.

In the fourth lesson, I tell the students that they are going to visit the library to obtain additional information. If the class is not proficient at note-making, it is important that help be given before proceeding. They should be introduced to a variety of methods for recording notes, e.g. using outlines, card systems, list formats, etc. In the first lesson, it is often useful to aid this process by providing printed sheets with separate sub-headings printed on each. In this way, students are given a simple format for recording information.

At this stage, I demonstrate note-making skills using a single reference book relevant to my topic. As I record the notes on the board or overhead projector, I talk to the students as follows:

> You'll notice how I don't write complete sentences. That's so I can record information quickly.
>
> Notice how I write the points in my own words.
>
> Sometimes I copy the exact words from the book because I can't say it another way. This is called a quote and is placed in quotation marks.
>
> Notice also that I copy down the exact spelling of unusual words. You can't check these easily in the dictionary later.

Don't forget to copy down the title of the book, and the author. This is called a reference and needs to be listed at the end of your report so everyone knows where your information came from.

For several lessons after this, the students are taken to the library to find out more about their topics. Again, if they are unfamiliar with the Dewey system or cannot use an index or table of contents, they must be shown how. Teachers need to be aware that many of the books children are asked to use have incomplete indexes (or none at all) and only brief outlines of content. This can prove a major stumbling block for students, and therefore they need to be taught coping strategies. It is important at this time to circulate among the students and employ the help of others if possible, e.g. the librarian.

During note-making the students are also encouraged to make sure their discovery draft statements are accurate. If so, they are added to their sheets in the relevant category. It is useful for teachers to demonstrate how this is done,

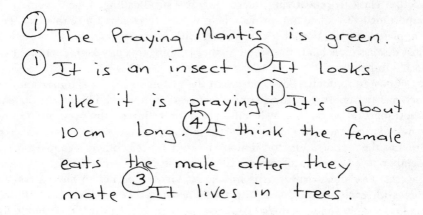

Fig. 9.2 A discovery draft that has been coded to demonstrate to students how information can be categorized under specific sub-headings.

using the discovery drafts modelled for the students. Also, it is important to have regular class sharing sessions during this research process. Have they experienced any problems? How did they solve them? Were some references more useful than others?

In the next lesson, I usually share my own notes and discuss the importance of the information. Have I included insignificant details? Is there overlap between the categories? Are there still gaps in my information? Have I repeated myself anywhere? I then demonstrate how these notes are turned into a cohesive portion of my final report. To do this, it is important to stress that the notes have been written in random order and that a more natural order is necessary.

One way of doing this is to read through the notes, numbering each point in the order in which they are to be incorporated into the text. I involve the class by discussing with them my decisions as I make them. Finally, I point out that these points need to be connected. I demonstrate how this is done and ask the class to repeat the process for one sub-heading. Once again, it is important to circulate and provide help where necessary. Once this has been completed, the section of text is shared with a partner and finally a general class discussion is held. In several further lessons, this process is replicated for each sub-heading.

Once the students have completed their draft reports, it is important that each has an opportunity to edit and proof-read their work. This can be done in a number of ways, but will reflect the procedures employed in writing generally in your classroom. For the editing of meaning, some teachers provide the opportunity for individual conferences, others group students together to go over draft material, others use buddy systems. In the early stages of research writing, it is important for the teacher to have a conference with each student, and to provide assistance where necessary. Proof-reading simply requires the students to check their own work thoroughly for spelling, punctuation and grammar. Once again, it can be done in a variety of ways, e.g. using individual and group conferences, parent helpers, partners, etc.

Once the students have completed their final draft it is time to talk about the presentation of their work. It is important to note that this only occurs after everything else has been done. At this stage, I usually show the class the completed reports of other students which have been published commercially. I point out the variations in format, the use of illustrations, maps, diagrams, etc. We discuss how these devices can be used and how important it is that they support the text. I always point out that illustrative material is not there just to make the work attractive – it is primarily to share additional information.

The students are then encouraged to come up with a plan for presenting their work, as well as a list of possible illustrative material. This should at least be shared with a partner and may also need to be discussed with the teacher.

Once their plans have been shared and approved, the students are ready to complete their final reports. This may take several lessons. Alternatively, some of the copying, illustrating and writing of headings might be done at home. The reports are then shared and displayed.

Variations to this strategy

As has already been stated, the process outlined in this chapter is only one of many formats. However, it is one which I have found useful. When choosing another format, it is important to ensure that the following essential features are maintained. The method chosen should:

1. Permit the integrated use of reading and writing.
2. Involve a repeated cycle of teacher modelling, discussion of real texts, jointly constructed texts, and pupil-controlled reading and writing (see Chapter 3 for more details).
3. Provide students with an opportunity to pursue a topic of interest within fairly broad parameters.
4. Permit students to help each other as part of the processes of reading and writing.
5. Provide opportunities for students to revise their work and negotiate meanings.

CHAPTER 10

Getting it all together: Integrating the reading and writing of literary texts

This chapter is concerned with integrated programmes for the reading of literary texts. Like Chapter 9, it attempts to show that the teaching of comprehension need not, and should not, occur as a series of decontextualized skills lessons. Rather, we need to find ways to help students elaborate the meanings they construct as they encounter whole texts. A complete literary reading programme requires the teacher to create an environment which provides opportunities for daily independent reading, spontaneous and structured responses to literature, and shared reading purely for enjoyment (Cairney, 1990). However, the focus of this book is comprehension. Hence my interest in this chapter is the development of integrated programmes that permit literature to be discussed, assessed, interpreted and criticized.

Approaches to programming

The sample programme that is provided on the following pages for the book *Charlotte's Web* (White, 1952), illustrates one way a framework can be provided for a structured response to literature (see Chapter 4). The approach adopted concentrates on the themes within the novel (i.e. major underlying messages that the author has attempted to communicate), plot characterization, structure, setting and language. Of the other approaches available, the following seem to be of most value:

1. *Genre (form) approach.* This approach has as its major focus features of a particular text genre (e.g. fables, fairy tales, legends, etc.). Using this approach, a teacher might plan a complete programme on Greek legends.
2. *Topic approach.* The teacher is required to choose books related to a specific topic, e.g. animal stories. This approach is less demanding in a literary sense, and is therefore arguably of less value for the development of

comprehension. Using this approach, a teacher might plan a programme based on adventure stories which have a horse as their major character.

3. *Structural approach*. This type of programme looks closely at the plot structure of the text(s). Narratives have a predictable plot structure, and can therefore be compared for their similarities or differences, or degrees of conformity to a particular structure. Teachers using this approach could plan a programme for examining a series of time-slip novels.

4. *Author studies*. These involve the study of several novels by the same writer. Normally, the programme starts with the teacher sharing details on the author. Following this, the class reads the novel closely to identify the particular features of the author's style. This approach can be used to study popular writers like Roald Dahl, but it proves most useful when it features more difficult writers like Leon Garfield, who often prove less popular with children.

Principles for programme development

The integrated programme which follows is based upon a number of important principles (from Cairney, 1990), but first it is essential to discuss the principles that have shaped the lessons outlined. These principles apply equally to all other programming approaches. The lessons planned should:

- never trivialize the meaning that authors, and for that matter readers, construct. For example, it would be trivial to plan a lesson on nuts because the mother in *Sounder* (Armstrong, 1971) used to shell nut kernels each night as she rocked in front of the fire. This would detract significantly from the major themes that the author has tried to develop (e.g. racism), the subtleties of the plot, language use, etc.;

- contain open comprehension tasks. That is, they should provide opportunities for students to have the potential meanings that they construct (as they meet the text) expanded, not narrowed. Open tasks permit multiple responses; closed tasks invite only one response;

- provide invitations to respond, not offer set tasks. There can be no guarantee that students will be interested in the teacher's suggestions for response to a piece of literature. To avoid this problem a choice should be provided. Rather than offering one task, it is better to suggest sufficient activities to permit students to choose something which captures their imagination;

- not contain forced integration. Our aim should be to plan comprehension activities which permit students to come to a greater understanding of the text. We should never set out to plan activities for all subjects without regard for the integrity of the book;

- provide comprehension tasks which promote the sharing of alternative responses to the text, not individual searches for the ideal meaning of the book;

* be a means of encouraging response to and the comprehension of text. We must avoid the trap of shifting the focus from the novel to the comprehension tasks.

Procedures for planning the programme

There are many possible ways to plan an integrated programme. However, I have found the following steps useful:

Step 1   Read the book without taking notes or planning any lessons.

Step 2   Re-read the book, looking for convenient break points or logical divisions which form lesson-sized sections that can be read in 10–15 minutes. The break points are then recorded so that the planning can begin.

Step 3   Scan the book again section by section, re-reading specific parts in detail and recording possible lesson ideas. This is essentially a brainstorming session. Ideas are recorded which focus on the underlying themes, characterization, plot, setting, language, form, etc.

Step 4   Re-read the rough notes, eliminating less desirable lessons and adding other ideas that emerge as the planning proceeds in more detail.

Step 5   Following this the lesson, content must be revised to ensure that each is of suitable length, difficulty, interest level, etc.

Step 6   Finally, the programme is re-read to ensure that each lesson fits logically into a total sequence and that each conforms to the above principles.

When reading the programme that follows, it is important to remember that it has been planned with a specific group of students (aged 10) and a particular context in mind. When planning programmes of this type, it is important to design them to match the needs of the class. The teacher needs to ask him or herself the vital question: 'What type of help do my students need to become more effective meaning makers?'

Not only does the content of these programmes vary, the format in which the literature is encountered may take a number of forms. For example, the book might be read to the class, a group of students might read the same novel silently chapter by chapter between planned lessons, or there may be a combination of teacher reading and independent reading. The programme that follows is dependent upon the teacher reading the story out loud to the class.

A sample programme for *Charlotte's Web*

Synopsis

Charlotte's Web (White, 1952) is a story of friendship, loyalty, life, death and hope. It tells of the relationship that develops between a spider (Charlotte) and a pig (Wilbur) as the threat of inevitable death disturbs the relative quiet of a country farmyard. Wilbur, a runt pig saved from death by Mr Arable's pleading daughter Fern, finds that as he grows up he still has a death sentence hanging over his head. But his life is changed by a chance meeting with Charlotte in the barnyard. The bond that grows between these two characters, and Charlotte's efforts to save Wilbur's life, are the sustaining forces of the story.

Aims of the programme

The major purposes for planning this programme are to help students to:

1. Become more aware of the themes of friendship, life, death, loyalty and hope raised in the book.
2. Appreciate the way White develops characters and portrays a richness of human qualities.
3. Project their own emotions into a story.
4. Examine the power of language to influence emotion.

Possible lessons

Lesson 1

Introduction   The purpose of this lesson is to engage the students in the story and encourage them to relate personal experiences to the book, and hence empathize with the main characters.

Procedure   Commence reading the book with little or no comment. At the end of Chapter 1, ask the class to break into groups of 3–5 students to discuss the following questions:

- What are your feelings towards Mr Arable? Was he justified in wanting to kill the pig? What arguments are there for and against his actions?
- Would you have reacted the way Fern did? Why or why not?

Bring the groups back together and ask an elected spokesperson to share some of their responses.

Read Chapter 2. After the reading, ask the class to share any experiences they have had raising small animals. What were their memories of the experience? How did they come to have the animal? How would they describe their relationship with the animal? Was it one of close 'friendship'? Can you be 'friends' with an animal?

Lesson 2

Introduction   The purpose of this lesson is to help students form a rich image of the barn and its surroundings in their minds. The aim is to help them see, hear, smell and feel the barn, and try to project themselves into the setting.

Procedure   Read Chapter 3. After the reading, allow the class time to offer general responses to the chapter. When the discussion has been allowed to proceed for a sufficient period of time, suggest to the class that they use sketch-to-stretch (see Chapters 4 and 5 for details) to show how they imagine the barn and its yard. If necessary, re-read the first few pages of the chapter. When the sketches have been done, provide an opportunity for the students to explain them to a neighbour.

Once the sketches have been completed, ask the students to find a partner to brainstorm words which describe the images they have of the barn and the yard. What are the sights, sounds, smells and tactile experiences that might be experienced if they were there? Share these as a class and compile a composite list of images.

Variations to this lesson   As a follow-up to the above activities, students might be encouraged to use their word images to write a poem about the barn. This could be done in free form or could follow a simple recipe format:

- write the title – 'The Barnyard';
- write 2 or 3 words which describe visual images;
- write 3 or 4 words which describe the sounds of the barn;
- write 3 or 4 words which describe the smells of the barn;
- write 2 or 3 words which express how you feel about the barn;
- write a synonym for barnyard.

Lesson 3

Introduction   The major purpose of this lesson is to focus the students' attention upon the theme of loneliness and the need to belong. Wilbur's depression provides a wonderful insight into this common human condition. Also, the class will be encouraged once again to empathize with Wilbur's situation and feelings.

Procedure   Read Chapter 4 to the class. After the reading, allow the students time to respond in general terms to the chapter. If necessary, ask questions which invite responses of a general nature: 'How did Wilbur's loneliness make you feel?' 'Do you think Wilbur's mysterious new friend will make a difference to his life?'

Following the initial discussion, focus the attention of the class upon the theme of loneliness. Why did Wilbur feel lonely? How did he react? Have you ever been lonely? Can you recall the reasons for your loneliness? What took your loneliness away?

As a conclusion to this lesson, invite the students to write a diary entry that Wilbur might have written (if he could write) at the end of the day. For example

> Well today has been quite a day. It started badly with rain, rain, rain. That was enough to depress anyone. The more I moped around, the more miserable I got. No-one in the farmyard wanted to have anything to do with me. Templeton was nowhere to be found at first, and then he turned up only to pinch my food. Fern didn't come near me, Goose was too busy sitting on eggs, and Lamb had better things to do. I was so depressed I couldn't even eat – goes to show how bad I was! To top it off, stupid Lurvy grabbed me and started shoving medicine down my throat – all I needed was a bit of love and attention. But just now something amazing happened, I found a brand new friend. I don't know what his or her name is, but tomorrow I'll know because this friend told me I'd find out in the morning. How exciting, a friend at last, I don't think I'll be able to sleep. Well I'd best try. Goodnight dear diary.

Show the class a sample entry for a character from another well-known book, and perhaps demonstrate the writing of a simple entry for another story that the class has shared.

Variations to this lesson Alternatives to the writing of a journal entry could include:

- Drawing a picture of Wilbur in his depressed state.
- Using sketch-to-stretch to draw the mysterious friend.
- Dramatizing one of the exchanges between Wilbur and the other farmyard characters.

Lesson 4

Introduction The major focus of this lesson is on the theme of friendship. At last Wilbur finds a friend in this chapter. This new friendship has a dramatic impact upon Wilbur's life. The class should be encouraged to relate Wilbur's experiences to their own lives, and to reflect upon the human need for friendship.

Procedure Read Chapter 5. After the chapter is read, break the class into groups of 3–5 students and ask them to discuss the following questions:

- What is Wilbur's reaction to his new friend? What are the things that he is surprised by, and doesn't like?

- How does Charlotte show friendship towards Wilbur?
- Have you ever met someone who at first you didn't find totally likeable because of his or her habits or personality? How did you both adjust to your differences?

After perhaps 10 minutes of discussion, invite the same groups to do a dramatic reading of the meeting between Wilbur and Charlotte. Commence where Charlotte greets Wilbur ('Salutations!') and end with Wilbur's statement that eating flies and bugs was a '. . . miserable inheritance'. Once the groups have had the opportunity to read this section, invite some of them to present their reading to the class.

As a culmination to the lesson, ask the students to discuss how this exchange illustrates the initial tentativeness of a new friendship, and the search for common ground. To start this discussion, the teacher might ask:

- What did Wilbur find hardest to accept about Charlotte?
- What might Charlotte have found hard to accept about Wilbur?

Variations to this lesson As an alternative activity, the teacher could invite his or her students to write a short poem entitled 'A Friend'. This poem could start with the words 'A Friend is', and be followed by a series of thoughts which indicate the true nature of friendship.

Lesson 5

Introduction The major purpose of this lesson is to consider Wilbur's sudden confrontation with death. This event changes the course of Wilbur's life and the story. A full discussion of the events that surround Wilbur's discovery is critical for the development of the plot.

Procedure Read Chapters 6 and 7. At the end of Chapter 7, ask the class to break into groups of 3–5 to discuss Wilbur's 'bad news'. What had he found out? How would he have felt? How did Wilbur react? Was this Wilbur's first awareness of his mortality? Would this have made it more or less traumatic?

Bring the students back together as a class and ask them to consider Charlotte's statement that she will save Wilbur. Ask the students to consider in their groups how Charlotte might achieve this. What type of plan could a spider devise to save the life of a pig?

Variations to this lesson It is possible to extend the discussion of death that this chapter raises to the lives of the students themselves. This is an extension that would need to be done very sensitively, and may not be dealt with at all with some classes. Following the discussion of Wilbur's rude awakening, the teacher might simply ask his or her students to discuss their first recollections of their own mortality. How did they feel? What made them aware that death is the natural culmination to life?

A further variation might be to give additional attention to the character Templeton. Although he is not a major character, many children relate well to him and would enjoy spending more time reflecting upon his character. To do this, the teacher could simply invite the class to prepare a character mug sheet for him (see Chapter 6).

Lesson 6

Introduction　The major focus within this lesson is the characters introduced into the story so far. White's farmyard characters in particular have a richness that few books manage to achieve. The class should be encouraged to consider the qualities of each of the major characters and to compare them on a number of personality traits.

Procedure　Read Chapters 8 and 9. Following the reading of both chapters, suggest to the class that *Charlotte's Web* contains a number of quite different characters. Ask the class to brainstorm a list of the farmyard characters, writing each name on the board as it is suggested. Once the list is complete, ask the class to reflect upon the personalities of each character. Suggest a series of traits (each of which has an opposite) and invite them to complete character rating scales (see Cairney, 1990) for each character (see Fig. 10.1).

The rating scales are completed by writing the names of each character at a point which it is felt represents the relative quality that he or she possesses. To do this, I usually break the class up into groups of 3–5 students and suggest that they negotiate their ratings. In using this strategy, it is assumed that the class has been introduced to this technique before, has seen it modelled, and has participated in the joint construction of several rating scales. It is important to point out to them that there are no right or wrong ratings for each of these scales. Explain that different readers will frequently assign different ratings for characters because they relate to them differently. Request that they simply try to reach consensus or apply a rating that is the mid-point of the group's views.

When the groups have completed the rating scales, a class scale is prepared that summarizes the overall views of the majority. This is done simply to enable all groups to share their views. When major differences emerge, it is important to ask the students to indicate why they have applied the rating that they have. It is important to remember that it is the discussion that takes place as the scales are prepared and the sharing sessions that follow that are of most importance. The completed scales have little value as products except as a record of the group's views, which, incidentally, tend to change as the story proceeds. A useful exercise is to compare the old ratings with perceptions of characters held at a later date.

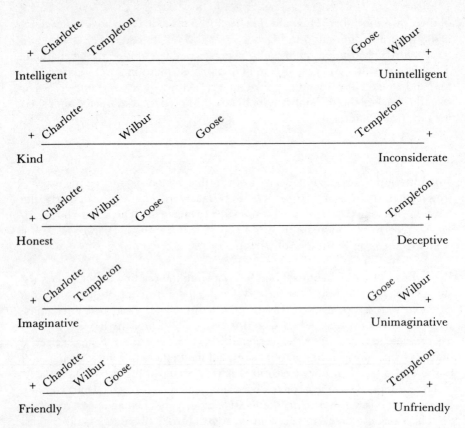

Fig. 10.1   Character rating scales for *Charlotte's Web* (White, 1952).

Variations to this lesson   A useful variation to this lesson is to allow the class to devise all, or some, of the personality traits to be used, and then complete the scales accordingly.

Lesson 7

Introduction   The purpose of this lesson is to encourage the students to reflect upon the events of Chapter 11 and consider the impact that such an incident might have if it occurred in real life.

Procedure   Read Chapters 10 and 11. At the conclusion of Chapter 11, provide the students with an opportunity to respond in general terms. If necessary, ask questions like the following: What do you think of Charlotte's solution to the problem? Do you think it will work? How would you have reacted if you had discovered the web?

After sufficient opportunity has been provided to respond, invite the class to write a newspaper article showing how a local newspaper might have reported the miraculous events on Zuckerman's farm. For example:

Literate Spider Stuns Everyone

A local farmer discovered to his amazement this morning that a spider living in his barn can spell. At first Mr Zuckerman could not believe his eyes. He found a large web in the doorway of his barn with the words SOME PIG clearly visible within its boundaries.

At first he thought it must have been a practical joke. However, local scientists have confirmed that the web is real, and could not have been made artificially. Experts are at a loss to explain the strange occurrence. They are even more baffled by the fact that there seems some connection between the message and a runt pig kept in the pen near the web.

The event has created incredible interest with local residents and within the scientific community. No-one knows whether this is an isolated event and observers will wait anxiously to see if it is repeated.

It is assumed that this technique would have been modelled in the past, and students would have been involved in the joint construction of newspaper articles. The students should be shown examples of newspaper articles and the teacher should discuss the features that distinguish this form of writing. Point out that newspaper reports normally answer the questions: Who? What? When? Where? Why? Once the articles have been written, they should be shared and displayed.

Variations to this lesson   As a variation to this lesson, students might choose to use other media for the reporting of events in Chapter 11. For example, they might:

- conduct a radio interview with Mr Zuckerman;
- act as an on-the-scene interviewer, talking to Zuckerman or Fern about the incident;
- prepare a written transcript of an interview between a witness to the event and a talk-back host for radio or television.

Lesson 8

Introduction   The major focus within this lesson is upon Charlotte's clever use of language. The discussion of the strategy used by Charlotte will be centred around the power of words. The students should be encouraged to experiment with language to create their own effects.

Procedure   Read Chapters 12 and 13 up to the point where Templeton begins a search of the dump for a newspaper clipping with a suitable word on it for Charlotte. Discuss the words that Charlotte has used so far. What has made these words so powerful? What are all the associations that people have been able to make with the words? What will be needed next time to catch everyone's attention?

Ask the students to break into groups of 3–5 and discuss some of the words they might use if given the opportunity. Provide bundles of old magazines and newspapers for students to search. Suggest that they cut words out, paste them on to a sheet and provide explanations for their choices. How would these words help save Wilbur's life?

After the groups have compiled their word banks, provide time for class sharing. Finally, the word banks should be displayed. Once the students have shared their work, complete the reading of Chapter 13.

Variations to this lesson The students could be invited to have fun with language by generating words which would have a negative impact upon people, e.g. delicious, mouth-watering, ginormous, etc.

Lesson 9

Introduction The major purpose of this lesson is to encourage the class to consider Charlotte's acknowledgement that she has little time left in which to help Wilbur. The students will also be asked to predict the events which might take place once Wilbur reaches the fair.

Procedure Read Chapters 14–16. Re-read the last paragraph of Chapter 15 in which it is revealed that Charlotte believes that 'she couldn't help Wilbur much longer', and that she would need to build an egg sac. Ask the students to form groups of 3–5 to discuss what this might mean. Why wouldn't she be able to help? Is the building of the egg sac connected with her inability to help for much longer? Following this discussion, ask the groups to report back to the whole class with their ideas.

As a conclusion to the lesson, ask the students to use sketch-to-stretch to represent their predictions about the events that will unfold in this story. What will happen at the fair? Will Charlotte try something else to save Wilbur's life?

Variations to this lesson Some classes might want to discuss the characteristics of a country fair. First-hand experience of such an event, by at least some of the students, would be necessary to allow this to take place. What is a fair like? What are the sights, sounds, smells and tastes that help to make the atmosphere of a fair unique?

Lesson 10

Introduction This lesson is mainly for reading. However, engagement in the story will be fostered by encouraging the students to make predictions following Charlotte's revelation in Chapter 18 concerning the 'special' surprise.

Procedure   Read Chapters 17–18. Following Chapter 18, ask the students to discuss the special thing that Charlotte is making for herself. What is it? What could be its purpose? Then read Chapter 19 and finish the lesson by discussing the accuracy of their predictions.

Lesson 11

Introduction   The purpose of this lesson is to encourage students to focus upon the death of Charlotte. The students will also be given the opportunity to empathize with Wilbur and discuss the impact that Charlotte's death might have on his life.

Procedure   Read Chapters 20–21. At the conclusion of Chapter 21 (in which Charlotte's death is revealed), provide opportunities for students to respond in their own way to the reading. After the students have had this opportunity, invite them to provide written responses in one of the following ways:

1. Write a diary entry for Wilbur following Charlotte's death.
2. Write about the death of someone or something (e.g. a pet) close to them that has been part of their experience.
3. Write the words of a poem or a song that Wilbur might have written in memory of Charlotte.
4. Prepare an epitaph that might have been written by Wilbur to appear on Charlotte's gravestone.

Complete the lesson by sharing the written work and reflecting upon the impact that death has upon the lives of those who are left behind.

Variations to this lesson   Some students might like to dramatize the dialogue that takes place with Wilbur when Charlotte reveals that she is going to die. This section of the text begins with Charlotte saying that she would 'not be going back to the barn' and ends with Wilbur crying 'If you're going to stay here I shall stay, too.'

In doing this, it is important to invite the students to consider why Wilbur reacts the way he does. Is he simply distraught for Charlotte, or is he concerned also for himself?

Lesson 12

Introduction   This lesson will initially provide students with an opportunity to respond generally to the complete novel. However, it also aims to encourage students to consider the cycle of life that the book illustrates – 'life goes on'. The students will also be encouraged to reflect upon the relationship between the major characters and the impact upon Wilbur of Charlotte's death.

Procedure   Read Chapter 22. Following the reading, provide an opportunity for students to offer general responses to the chapter. If necessary, ask questions like: Did you like the ending? How did it make you feel? Did it remind you of any other books? Why?

    After this discussion, encourage the students to reflect upon the hatching of Charlotte's children. What did their birth signify?

    Ask the class to form groups of 3–5 students to discuss the relationship between Wilbur and Charlotte. Encourage them to come up with a list of the five most important aspects of the relationship between them. What were the major reasons for the special nature of their relationship? After sufficient time has been allowed for this discussion, ask the groups to share their ideas. Compile a master list of the 10 reasons cited most frequently by the groups.

Conclusions   As a conclusion to this lesson, the teacher could share with his or her students other books that have also raised the themes of friendship, loyalty, life, death and companionship. Books that might be considered are:

* *The Pinballs* by Betsy Byars (1977).
* *Summer of My German Soldier* by Bette Greene (1974).
* *Granpa* by John Burningham (1980).
* *The Great Gilly Hopkins* by Katherine Paterson (1978b).
* *Bridge to Terabithia* by Katherine Paterson (1978a).
* *My Sister Sif* by Ruth Park (1986).

A final word

I began this book by pointing out that it was not typical of the books published previously on reading comprehension. I have attempted to challenge the traditional information transfer definitions of comprehension and teaching, and have endeavoured to redefine the roles of the teacher and learner in a reading classroom. In the process, I have outlined classroom practices that are consistent with my stated beliefs. All of these strategies work in classrooms; I know because I have used them. However, being able to say something 'works' is not sufficient justification for its continued use. There are many definitions of what 'works'. For some, a teaching practice works if it keeps students gainfully employed for long periods of time. For others, satisfaction is gained and a feeling of success experienced if students display any number of behaviours as a result of instruction. Frequently, these behaviours are related purely to the task set and have limited relevance to learning in the real world.

It is my belief that the only criteria that matter when attempting to justify the use of any reading strategy are as follows:

1. Is the reader a better meaning-maker as a result of his or her involvement in this learning experience?
2. Does the learning experience lead to a more enthusiastic desire to read for a range of purposes?
3. Are students using reading for purposes other than those defined by the school? Are they reading outside school?
4. Is reading becoming a significant part of the students' worlds?

My hope is that readers of this book will structure their classroom environments in such a way that these questions can be answered in the affirmative for all students. Teachers face many great challenges in the 1990s. One of the most significant must surely be the need to reshape reading curricula in such a way that more students discover they can use reading for purposes which they see as significant for themselves. If this book has helped in any way to achieve this aim for your students, then its primary purpose has been realized.

Bibliography

Anderson, R.C. and Biddle, W.B. (1975). On asking people questions about what they are reading. In G.H. Bower (Ed.), *The Psychology of Learning and Motivation*, Vol. 9. London: Academic Press.

Atwell, N.A. (1983). Reading, writing, speaking, listening: Language in response to context. In V. Hardt (Ed.), *Teaching Reading with the Other Language Arts*. Delaware: International Reading Association.

Bakhtin, M. (1929). *Problems of Dostoevsky's Poetics* (translated by R.W. Rotsel, 1973). Ann Arbor: Ardis.

Barrett, T. (1976). Taxonomy of reading comprehension. In R. Smith and T.C. Barrett, *Teaching Reading in the Middle Grades*. Reading, Mass.: Addison-Wesley.

Beck, I.L., McKeown, M.G., McCaslin, E.S. and Burkes, A.M. (1979). *Instructional Dimensions that may Affect Reading Comprehension: Examples from Two Commercial Reading Programs*. Pittsburgh: University of Pittsburgh, Learning Research and Development Center.

Bleich, D. (1978). *Subjective Criticism*. Baltimore: Johns Hopkins University Press.

Bloom, B.S. (1956). *Taxonomy of Educational Objectives, Handbook I: Cognitive Domain*. New York: David McKay.

Bloome, D. (1985). Reading as a social process. *Language Arts*, **62** (2).

Boyer, E. (1984). *High School: A Report on American Secondary Education*. New York: Harper and Row.

Brown, H. and Cambourne, B. (1987). *Read and Retell*. Sydney: Methuen.

Bruner, J. (1983). *Child's Talk: Learning to Use Language*. Oxford: Oxford University Press.

Bruner, J. (1986). *Actual Minds, Possible Worlds*. Cambridge, Mass.: Harvard University Press.

Cairney, T.H. (1983). *Balancing the Basics*. Sydney: Ashton Scholastic.

Cairney, T.H. (1985a). *Users, Not Consumers of Language: One Class Takes Control of its Own Learning*. Proceedings of the 11th Australian Reading Conference, Brisbane, 4–7 July.

Cairney, T.H. (1985b). Linking reading and writing. In D. Burnes, H. French and F. Moore (Eds), *Literacy: Strategies and Perspectives*. Adelaide: ARA.

Cairney, T.H. (1986). *Helping Children to Make Meaning – Ten Literature-based Activities for Developing Literacy*. Wagga Wagga: Riverina Literacy Centre.

Cairney, T.H. (1987a). The social foundations of literacy. *Australian Journal of Reading*, **10** (2).

Cairney, T.H. (1987b). *Developing Literature-based Literacy Programmes: Getting Kids 'Inside' Books*. Wagga Wagga: Riverina Literacy Centre.

Cairney, T.H. (1987c). *Literature-based Programmes*. Wagga Wagga: Riverina Literacy Centre.

Cairney, T.H. (1987d). Teaching reading comprehension: The development of critical and creative readers. *Australian Journal of Reading*, **11** (3).

Cairney, T.H. (1988a). Perceptions of basal reading materials: Children have their say. *The Reading Teacher*, **41** (4).

Cairney, T.H. (1988b). Teaching reading comprehension: The development of critical and creative readers. *Australian Journal of Reading*, **11** (3).

Cairney, T.H. (1989). *Composing Meaning: Writing and Reading the Complex Fabric of Text*. Paper presented to the joint conference of the Australian Reading Association and Australian Association for the Teaching of English, Darwin, 30 June to 4 July.

Cairney, T.H. (1990). *Other Worlds: The Endless Possibilities of Literature*. Sydney: Martin Educational.

Cairney, T.H. and Langbien, S. (1989). Building communities of readers and writers. *The Reading Teacher*, **42** (8).

Carner, R.L. (1963). Levels of questioning. *Education*, **83**.

Chapman, L.J. (1979). The perception of language cohesion during fluent reading. In P.A. Kolers, M. Wrolstad and H. Bouma (Eds), *Processing of Visible Language*. New York: Plenum.

Chapman, L.J. (1983). *Reading Development and Cohesion*. London: Heinemann.

Collerson, J. (Ed.) (1988). *Writing for Life*. Sydney: PETA.

Corcoran, B. and Evans, E. (Eds) (1987). *Readers, Texts, Teachers*. Upper Montclair, N.J.: Boynton/Cook.

Dewey, J. and Bentley, L. (1949). *Knowing and the Known*. Boston: Beacon.

Dillon, J.T. (1982). The multidisciplinary study of questioning. *Journal of Educational Psychology*, **74** (2).

Durkin, D. (1978–9). What classroom observations reveal about reading comprehension instruction. *Reading Research Quarterly*, **XIV**, 481–537.

Flanders, N.A. (1970). *Analyzing Teaching Behaviour*. Reading, Mass.: Addison-Wesley.

Freire, P. and Macedo, D. (1987). *Literacy: Reading the Word and the World*. London: Routledge and Kegan Paul.

Gall, M. (1970). The use of questions in teaching. *Review of Educational Research*, **40** (5).

Giroux, H. (1983). *Theory and Resistance in Education*. London: Heinemann.

Good, T.L. and Brophy, J.E. (1978). *Looking in Classrooms*. New York: Harper and Row.

Goodlad, J. (1983). *A Place Called School*. New York: McGraw-Hill.

Goodman, K. (1982). Reading: A psycholinguistic guessing game. In F. Gollasch (Ed.), *Language & Literacy*. Boston: Routledge and Kegan Paul.

Goodman, K. (1984). Unity in reading. *Becoming Readers in a Complex Society: 83rd*

Yearbook of the National Society for the Study of Education (Part 1). Chicago: University of Chicago Press.

Gough, P. (1972). One second of reading. In J.F. Kavanaugh and I.G. Mattingly (Eds), *Language by Ear and by Eye*. Cambridge, Mass.: MIT Press.

Gough, P. (1985) One second of reading: Postscript. In H. Singer and R.B. Ruddell (Eds), *Theoretical Models and Processes of Reading*, 3rd edn. Newark: International Reading Association.

Graves, D. (1983). *Writing: Teachers & Children at Work*. Exeter, New Hampshire: Heinemann.

Graves, M.F. and Clark, D.L. (1981). The effect of adjunct questions on high school low achievers' reading comprehension. *Reading Improvement*, **18**.

Gray, B. (1987). How natural is 'natural' language teaching – employing wholistic methodology in the classroom. *Australian Journal of Education*, **12** (4).

Halliday, M.A.K. (1975). *Learning How to Mean: Explorations in the Development of Language*. London: Edward Arnold.

Harding, D.W. (1972). The role of onlooker. In A. Cashdan (Ed.), *Language in Education: A Source Book*. Milton Keynes: Open University Press.

Harste, J.C. (1985). Portrait of a new paradigm: Reading comprehension research. In A. Crismore (Ed.), *Landscapes: A State-of-the-Art Assessment of Reading Comprehension Research (1974–1984)*. Final report of US Department of Education funded project USDEC-C-300-83-0130, Indiana University.

Harste, J.C., Woodward, V. and Burke, C. (1984). *Language Stories and Literacy Lessons*. Dover, New Hampshire: Heinemann.

Harste, J.C., Pierce, K. and Cairney, T.H. (1985). *The Authoring Cycle: A Viewing Guide*. Dover, New Hampshire: Heinemann.

Hoetker, J. and Ahlbrand, W.P. (1969). The persistence of the recitation. *American Educational Research Journal*, **6**.

Holdaway, D. (1979). *The Foundations of Literacy*. Sydney: Ashton Scholastic.

Holland, N. (1975). *Five Readers Reading*. New Haven, Conn.: Yale University Press.

Hopkins, H. (1978). *Clozing the Gaps*. Wagga Wagga: Riverina Literacy Centre.

Hyman, R.T. (1979). *Strategic Questionning*. Englewood Cliffs, N.J.: Prentice-Hall.

Iser, W. (1978). *The Act of Reading: A Theory of Aesthetic Response*. Baltimore: Johns Hopkins University Press.

Johnson, T. and Louis, D. (1985). *Literacy through Literature*. Sydney: Methuen.

La Berge, D. and Samuels, S.J. (1985). Toward a theory of automatic information processing in reading. In H. Singer and R.B. Ruddell (Eds), *Theoretical Models and Processes of Reading*, 3rd edn. Newark: International Reading Association.

McGaw, B. and Grotelueschen, A. (1972). Direction of the effect of questions in prose material. *Journal of Educational Psychology*, **63**.

Markle, G. and Capie, W. (1976). The effect of the position of inserted questions on learning from an activity centred science module. *Journal of Research in Science Teaching*, **13** (2).

Meek, M. (1982). *Learning to Read*. London: Bodley Head.

Morris, B. and Stewart-Dore, N. (1984). *Learning to Learn from Text*. Sydney: Addison-Wesley.

Moyer, J.R. (1965). *An Exploratory Study of Questioning in the Instructional Processes in Selected Elementary Schools*. Unpublished doctoral dissertation, Columbia University, Ann Arbor, Mich. University Microfilms, 66–2661.

Mullis, I., Applebee, A. and Langer, J. (1986). *National Assessment of Educational Progress Report*, Washington DC: US State Department of Health, Education and Welfare, November.

National Assessment of Educational Progress Committee (1981). Reading comprehension. *Education Today*, 16 November.

Painter, C. (1986). The role of interaction in learning to speak and learning to write. In C. Painter and J. Martin (Eds), *Writing to Mean: Teaching Genres Across the Curriculum*. Applied Linguistics Association of Australia, Occasional Papers, No. 9.

Palincsar, A. and Brown, A. (1983). *Reciprocal Teaching of Comprehension-monitoring Activities*, Technical Report No. 269. Urbana, Ill.: Center for the Study of Reading.

Pearson, P.D. and Johnson, D.D. (1978). *Teaching Reading Comprehension*. New York: Holt, Rinehart and Winston.

Peirce, C.S. (1966). *Collected Papers of Charles Sanders Peirce*. Boston: Belknap Press.

Piaget, J. (1966). *The Psychology of Intelligence*. Totowa, N.J.: Littlefield, Adams and Co.

Rickards, J.P. and Hatcher, C.W. (1976). Type of verbatim question interspersed in text: A new look at the position effect. *Journal of Reading Behaviour*, **8**.

Rosenblatt, L. (1978). *The Reader, the Text, the Poem*. Carbondale: Southern Illinois University Press.

Rosenblatt, L. (1985). The transactional theory of literary work: Implications for research. In C.R. Cooper (Ed.), *Researching Response to Literature and the Teaching of Literature: Points of Departure*. Norwood, N.J.: Ablex.

Rothkopf, E.Z. (1966). Learning from written instructive materials: An exploration of the control of inspection behaviour by test-like events. *American Educational Research Journal*, **3**.

Rothkopf, E.Z. (1972). Structural text features and the control of processes in learning from written materials. In R.O. Freedle and J.B. Carroll (Eds), *Language Comprehension and the Acquisition of Knowledge*. Washington, D.C.: Winston.

Rowe, D. (1984). *Reading Comprehension Instruction: A 'Guided Tour' of Research (1974-1984)*. Paper presented to National Reading Council Conference, Florida, 1-4 December.

Shanklin, N. (1982). *Relating Reading and Writing: Developing a Transactional Theory of the Writing Process*. Bloomington, Ind.: Indiana University Press.

Short, K. (1986). *Literacy as a Collaborative Experience*. Unpublished doctoral dissertation, Indiana University, Bloomington, Ind.

Sizer, T. (1984). *A Study of High Schools*. New York: Houghton Mifflin.

Smith, F. (1978). *Reading Without Nonsense*. New York: Teachers College Press.

Smith, F. (1988). *The Literacy Club*. London: Heinemann.

Smith, N.B. (1963). *Reading Instruction for Today's Children*. Englewood Cliffs, N.J.: Prentice-Hall.

Snow, C.E. (1983). Literacy and language: Relationships during the preschool years. *Harvard Educational Review*, **53** (2).

Stauffer, R.G. (1969). *Directing the Reading-Thinking Process*. New York: Harper and Row.

Stevens, R. (1912). The question as a measure of efficiency in instruction: A critical study of classroom practice. *Teachers' College Contributions to Education*, **48**.

Thomson, J. (1987). *Understanding Teenagers' Reading: Reading Processes and the Teaching of Literature*. Melbourne: Methuen.

Tierney, R.J. and Cunningham, J.W. (1984). Research on teaching reading comprehension. In P.D. Pearson, R. Barr, M.L. Kamil and P. Mosenthal (Eds), *Handbook of Reading Research*. New York: Longman.

Van Allen, R. (1961). *Report of the Reading Study Project*. Monograph No. 1. San Diego: Department of Education.

Vygotsky, L. (1978). *Mind in Society: The Development of Higher Psychological Processes*. M. Cole, S. Scribner, V. John-Steiner and E. Souderman (Eds). Cambridge, Mass.: Harvard University Press.

Watson, D. (1985). Estimate, read, respond, question. In A. Crismore (Ed.), *Landscapes: A State-of-the-Art Assessment of Reading Comprehension Research, 1974–1984*. Final report of US Department of Education funded project, USDEC-C-300-83-0130, Indiana University.

Wells, G. (1986). *The Meaning Makers*. Dover, New Hampshire: Heinemann.

Wiesendanger, K.D. and Wollenberg, J.P. (1978). Prequestioning inhibits third grader's reading comprehension. *The Reading Teacher*, **31** (9).

Wilen, W.W. (1982). *What Research Says to the Teacher – Questioning Skills for Teachers*. New York: National Education Association.

Children's publications

Adams, P. (1973). *There was an Old Lady Who Swallowed a Fly*. Purton: Child's Play.
Armstrong, W. (1971). *Sounder*. London: Victor Gollancz.
Byars, B. (1977). *The Pinballs*. London: Bodley Head.
Burningham, J. (1973). *Mr Gumpy's Motor Car*. London: Jonathan Cape.
Burningham, J. (1980). *Granpa*. London: Jonathan Cape.
Carle, E. (1970). *The Very Hungry Caterpillar*. London: Hamish Hamilton.
Carroll, P. (1980). Ned Kelly. *Challenge*, 5, 3–4.
Dahl, R. (1967). *Charlie and the Chocolate Factory*. London: George Allen & Unwin.
Dahl, R. (1982). *The BFG*. London: Jonathan Cape.
Dahl, R. (1984). *Boy*. London: Jonathan Cape.
Eastman, P.D. (1960). *Are You My Mother?*. New York: Random House.
Eastman, P.D. (1968). *The Best Nest*. New York: Random House.
Education Department of Victoria (1980). Raising the Titanic. *Explore*, 6, 12–13.
Garfield, L. (1981). *Fair's Fair*. London: Macdonald Futura.
Garfield, L. (1985). *The Wedding Ghost*. Oxford: Oxford University Press.
Grahame, K. (1908). *The Wind in the Willows*. London: Methuen.
Greene, B. (1974). *Summer of My German Soldier*. London: Hamish Children's Books.
Heide, F.P. (1975). *The Shrinking of Treehorn*. Harmondsworth: Penguin.
Hutchins, P. (1978). *Don't Forget the Bacon*. London: Bodley Head.
Jacobs, J. (1969). Three little pigs. In B. Sideman (Ed.), *The World's Best Fairy Stories*. Sydney: Reader's Digest.
Lang, A. (1969). Jack and the beanstalk. In B. Sideman (Ed.), *The World's Best Fairy Stories*. Sydney: Reader's Digest.
Lawson, H. (1970). *The Loaded Dog*. Sydney: Angus and Robertson.
McClintock, M. (1958). *A Fly Went By*. New York: Random House.
Munsch, R. (1980). *The Paper Bag Princess*. Toronto: Annick Press.
Park, R. (1986). *My Sister Sif*. Sydney: Viking Kestrel.
Paterson, A.B. (1976). *A Bush Christening*. Sydney: Collins.
Paterson, K. (1978a). *Bridge to Terabithia*. London: Victor Gollancz.
Paterson, K. (1978b). *The Great Gilly Hopkins*. New York: T.Y. Crowell.
Pavey, P. (1981). *One Dragon's Dream*. Harmondsworth: Penguin.
Townsend, S. (1983). *The Secret Diary of Adrian Mole Aged 13¾ Years*. London: Methuen.

Verne, J. (1954). *Twenty Thousand Leagues Under the Sea*. New York: Simon and Schuster.

Viorst, J. (1973). *Alexander and the Terrible, Horrible, No Good, Very Bad Day*. London: Angus and Robertson.

Watanabe, S. (1979). *How Do I Eat It?* Tokyo: Fukuinkan Shoten.

White, E.B. (1952). *Charlotte's Web*. New York: Harper and Row.

Wilhelm, H. (1985). *I'll Always Love You*. New York: Crown.

Index